Through The Eyes Of A Therapist

IAN BEST

Copyright © 2015 by Ian Stuart Best

All rights reserved. This book or any portion thereof
may not be reproduced or used in any manner whatsoever
without the express written permission of the publisher
except for the use of brief quotations in a book review.

Printed in the United States of America

First Printing 2015

ISBN 9781 500 596 552

Dedicated to ......

Dedicated to all the people who have allowed me the privilege of being alongside them not only in their struggles and pain but also in their discoveries, their growth, their liberation and the unveiling of their futures!

Thank you.....

Thank you to all the many people who have contributed over the years to shaping me as a therapist and a person.

Thank you to my family, my friends and my wife Claire especially for her unswerving loyalty to me, which seems to know no bounds.

About the Author

Ian Best is a Psychotherapist based in the UK.
He is the director and founder of the exclusive therapy company *Total Therapeutics*. He is a supremely motivated, passionate and extremely enthusiastic man who simply wants the best for others and for them to live the life they were destined to!

Over the years he has been influenced by many eminent therapists and found R.D. Laing, Eric Berne, Aaron Beck and Carl Rogers to be amongst the most significant to him.

His work includes treating people with various forms of anxiety, phobias, low esteem, relationship issues and other forms of emotional difficulties. He also works with those who have sadly experienced trauma such as those who have worked in the military, victim of an attack or been involved in road traffic accidents.

He is a champion of empowering others and believes wholeheartedly in the liberation of choices, autonomy and taking control of the direction of our lives.

With Ian's help people with a range of concerns and difficulties discover, within themselves, the potential to change and become empowered.

A former professional pianist he continues to write, compose and perform at this current time.

Total Therapeutics

At Total Therapeutics we are completely devoted to enabling you to make the very, very best of yourself and overcoming all that may be holding you back.

We produce first class, rapid and long lasting results that you will serve you, your family and your life for years and years to come.

We will be with you all the way and stop at nothing from getting you to where you want to be!

We can help with anxiety, depression, trauma, low confidence, panic, phobias, relationship difficulties and most personal issues.

Visit us and see more about all of our superb products and services at www.totaltherapeutics.co.uk.

You can also find out more and contact Ian at

www.ian.best

www.totaltherapeutics.co.uk

Preface

The content of this book comes from extensive work on the cutting edge of personal therapeutic experience. It also comes from being allowed to witness the turbulent and the joyous, the brutal and the beautiful and also the resilience of people that beggars belief.

It could not have happened without so many people baring their souls and being brave enough to confront their pain, shame and distress.

So many people have surrendered to vulnerability and then gone onto realise the power that it actually has and used this as source of power to jettison them back on course.

It takes bravery to be a Therapist for many reasons mostly because you never know from one minute to the next what might happen, what somebody might say or what you might then say back to them. However, it takes greater bravery still to sit in the chair opposite a Therapist. So, here's to the brave, the vulnerable and to you!

May this book and the words in the pages give you the spark you need to become a roaring inferno!

Chapters

Introduction p.10

Chapter One p.20
Tolerance & Awareness

Chapter Two p.35
So, what is wrong with me?

Chapter Three p.47
The K.I.S.S. Theory

Chapter Four p.56
The Rule Book

Chapter Five p.66
The Bottle of Pop

Chapter Six p.81
Uncertainty

Chapter Seven p.93
Blame and Expectations

Chapter Eight p.108
Depression? Anxiety?

Chapter Nine p.119
Obstacles and Toolboxes

Chapter Ten p.131
Always Hope

Introduction

"I would also like you to know that I am fully convinced that the human spirit and soul are resilient beyond belief……"

Introduction

So, yes, I'm a Psychotherapist and whenever this gets raised in conversation it usually brings up a mixture of responses.

This ranges from confusion, *"So, what is it that you actually do then?"*

Cynicism, *"Huh, how are you able to help people?"*

Curiosity, "I bet you see some interesting people".

The optimistic, *"It must feel great to know that you are helping".*

The jokey, *"Ooo, can you tell me what all my problems are then?"*

The concerned, *"Have you been psycho-analysing me all this time?"*

And the evergreen, *"Don't you feel suicidal with everybody telling you their problems all day?"*

By the way, I can answer the final enquiry with a sincere and emphatic no and I hope that you will pick up throughout this book what a privilege I feel it is to do this work.

So the notion of being a therapist and what a therapist

does seems to generate a broader range of reactions from others which may not be the case with most other professions.

Ok, so what do I do? Well, I endeavour to help people overcome fears, doubts, anxieties, concerns, loss, confusion, trauma, transitions, insecurities, low esteem and woeful confidence and many, many other issues. Enabling them to move through these phases and episodes so that they can live more fully, freely and faithful to themselves.

Interestingly, though, virtually every patient I have ever seen has told me at some point or other they feel that everybody else manages just fine telling me how "they look ok" and "they all seem to be dealing with things much better than I am." I am rarely believed, though, when I tell people that in my experience this is just not the case. Comments like that are usually connected with the levels of expectations that people place on themselves and at this point the debilitating word 'should' usually puts in an appearance.

People can find major empowerment, though, from realising that actually it isn't just them who struggle with X, Y or Z, yet the vast majority are convinced that really it is only them who isn't good, strong, capable, competent or adequate enough to overcome whatever it is that they find themselves experiencing.

I can say for sure, no matter what people think or feel, it isn't the case that everybody else manages just fine. Not convinced? Well, for one it just can't be the case as otherwise all the therapists, coaches, teachers, priests etc in the world would be out of work. The never ending shelves of self-help books, guidance and also the abundance of "information" that there is online and in the shops would not be there and more so I would not be writing this.

Besides that, if it were true then the waiting lists at all the therapy centres would be blank pieces of paper. All the solicitors and insurance companies involved with helping people overcome struggles, accidents and traumas in life would be out of business and universities and colleges would not be training more therapists. Also, if it were true that people managed just fine then surely they would be dancing in the streets, throwing parties, starting revolutions and preaching the joys of life at the top of their voices.

Alongside this it does seem to be quite a sad and unfortunate trait of most people in that they are extremely reluctant to accept that their feelings are justified. More importantly, to ask for help particularly at times when they are in the most pain, distress or upset. I see people relentlessly attempt to dig deeper and deeper into a virtually already empty tank. Trying to battle through like a worn out one man band who is hampered by completely unhelpful beliefs such as:

"Everybody else seems to manage ok"

"I don't want to bother people"

"Nobody would be interested in my problems"

and the timeless classic

"There is always somebody worse off than me".

Let me just say right now though, I have at times said, felt and thought most of the above. If I am going to be completely honest with you I too have tried to battle on under my own steam and trudged through numerous personal wars and horror stories without asking for help. I am quite reluctant to talk about my own struggle's as I don't want to de-focus from the purpose of this book, although, I feel I can tell you that I have known quite a few ups and downs. I was born with quite limiting physical disabilities that continue to make life problematic to this day, I have unfortunately been through divorce, debt, been fired, seen business investments crash and both my parents died when I was quite young, one through suicide.

So I feel that it is not only my own professional experience that gives me understanding and appreciation of the pain and suffering that others go through but also my own personal experience of life that has so far contained paralysing lows yet also incredible highs, all of which are extremely memorable. I guess that if you're reading this book you can at some level relate to finding life harder than you would prefer it to be. You might feel that you want to be more, maybe you are unhappy with how things are, there could be something you want to consign to the past or you are looking for the access code that will set you free.

So, forgive me for assuming that we may at least have something in common either now or in the past but I am going to. Experiences that you and I may have had that we would like to forget, instances that left deep emotional scars, being attacked (I don't mean physically) by others and looking in the mirror and not recognising the person that looked back at us.

I wish I could tell you that I overcame my own issues and struggles in a streamlined way and that I was able to apply balanced thinking to move me on and that I did the right things at the right time and was able to self-heal and confer compassion onto myself but, you guessed it, I can't. Instead I hauled my head and heart around trying to fathom things out and make sense of my world, yet not in a very productive way at all. I can remember feeling completely stranded at the loss of relationships that left me emotionally bereft and extremely empty. I had to cancel work and plans due to not being able to face the day and wondering why life just seemed to be getting harder and not easier.

I did overcome these experiences through sheer heartfelt force, digging deeper than I ever thought possible and yes, I'll say this also, just battling through. Yet, I more than cringe to acknowledge that now and it is the type of method and approach that I would empathically challenge should a patient of mine make a similar claim or comment.

These experiences are something that I don't really reflect on these days, although at times some things do come back to haunt me, lately I have other battles that seem more emotionally sophisticated, subtle and disabling.

So I have my own personal struggles to tap into and many, many thousands of hours of having the honour of being alongside others who are struggling. Has all of this taught me anything about how we can tie ourselves up in knots, anything about how we can make life so much harder than it needs to be, how we can place limits, barriers and restrictions on ourselves? The answer of course is yes, I hope!

I feel that all of these precious experiences have given me an education that you can't buy, that you can't study for, something that can only be acquired by being alongside the struggles and challenges of others.

I have felt beyond grateful to have been allowed to know and hear so many thousands of peoples darkest fears, their most painful moments and tens of thousands of disclosures that would humble and embarrass the longest standing Priest.

I hope that due to this I may be able to give you insight, guidance, encouragement and empowerment to move on, become more and discard habits, thoughts and behaviours that simply are not doing you any favours at all.

I would also like you to know that I am fully convinced

that the human spirit and soul are resilient beyond belief and that there is, inbuilt within us, a relentless force that will somehow fight back despite dreadful conditions, treatment and suffering. I have seen, literally right before my eyes, people recover from the deepest darkest depths and such awful treatment at the hands of others and equally awful self-imposed suffering and pain. I have seen this not just once but thousands of times.

There is, I believe, a never ever say die force which is hard wired within us that refuses to give up irrespective of distress, loss, trauma and violence towards us. It is a mind blowing voice and strength that I have seen lift people out of horrific lows and bleakness to return to a point where they can say that they have overcome the pain and the hurt. This is often followed by the realisation that they are much stronger than they thought which is always a truly magical moment.

You might gather that I feel that there is always hope - there always is. I also believe that people can triumph over the most challenging adversity, however, a readiness for change is the real key. I have equally seen empowered and liberated individuals fall back into patterns and downward spirals that led them to struggle and seek help in the first place and many people just unable to take the first step of faith. Yet I have no doubt at all that when hope is accompanied by an open mind and an attitude that is ready to embrace change and growth, well, the world had better watch out as that's when the awesome power of the human condition kicks in and kicks ass!

The examples and much of the content in this book

comes from the coal face of the therapy room, from real life instances of what people do or have done when the going has, to say the least, gotten tough. I also want to impress upon you that despite what I may express at times in these pages, please do not think that I am in any way down on people. Nothing could be further from the truth, I am super up on people! I place immense importance on boosting others, empowering everybody I can and projecting positive energy into the world.

This book is intentionally not the most scientific or the most academic or an instruction manual as such. I have written about relentlessly common themes that I have seen thousands of times and the unfortunate and often avoidable trials and tribulations that people needlessly endure.

I hope that you will find in these pages uplifting messages and motivation that will give you the get out of jail card that you might have been searching for. Also I wanted this book to be accessible and user friendly as I also believe that you and I can be liberated with the assistance of the simplistic, the smallest of words or gestures and of course the phenomenal power within.

More than anything, as a result of reading, this book I truly want you to tap into your potential that may currently be lying dormant and stagnating so that you become more, become bigger, better, bolder, but above all that you become you.

THROUGH THE EYES OF A THERAPIST

Chapter One

Tolerance & Awareness

"Although on the other hand our ability to tolerate so much can contribute to our gradual undoing and there can be a downside to it……."

Chapter One
Tolerance & Awareness

Over the years I have owned one or two "nicer" cars but still nothing in the super car class and nothing flashier than a mid-range Ford or Vauxhall. I did once feel especially proud though to own a Ford Orion in bright red, it was a little older but it was in very good condition and was very eye catching. I adopted my usual I've got a new car plan and made a deal with myself to wash it regularly and keep it clean on the inside too. Alongside this I told myself I would check the oil and water levels frequently. On one particular day I was struck with a piece of (what seemed at the time) genius thinking, I would put plenty of oil in the engine and it would run brilliantly! I didn't of course realise at that time that it's possible to put too much oil in your car's engine!

Two or three days later I was completely baffled to notice that my car had developed an oil leak, a very slight drip, drip, drip onto the road. I was bemused at how this could be? I had put plenty of oil in the car. A relative who was a mechanic diagnosed things very quickly and told me that I had, ignorantly, put too much oil in the car. Too much oil I queried? How is this possible? You can put too much oil in a car? I was informed that too much oil had reduced the space needed in the engine block and that the pressure in the engine had built up so much (due to the reduced space) that the tiniest pinprick of a hole in a gasket had been found as an escape route for the pressure, and the oil!

This true experience has real comparisons for our lives if you compare yourself to a car and compare the pressures, demands and stresses that we can place on ourselves with the oil. Yet, despite people's concerted efforts and best intentions to keep the car running ok more oil gets poured into the engine (it will run ok right?) and more and more until people are surprised, just like me, that they develop a "leak". Then they need a "mechanic" to help figure out the problem and to help them correct it. Although, just as I was baffled, I see people equally confused at how the wheels appear to have come off their wagon.

So, what is this all due to? Well, allow me to introduce you to our great friend and enemy, tolerance. Tolerance can be such a blessing and a nemesis too. For example, if somebody wants to lift weights, run further or faster or extend their concentration span, increasing tolerance is the key to these efforts and is essential for progress to be made. Although, on the other hand, our ability to tolerate so much can contribute to our gradual undoing and there can be a downside to it.

The shoes I have to wear are made quite specifically due to the shape of one of my feet, this means I can't just buy them off the shelf and I also need to wear them until they are really quite old, worn and scuffed, as new pairs are limited. When I do get a new pair of shoes I still hold off from wearing them until I hate my old shoes so much that I just can't bear to wear them anymore.
In the split second that I put my new shoes on it hits me, I realise immediately how really uncomfortable and

unsupportive my old pair had become.

Had I realised this as I had gone along though? No of course not. Why? Because my tolerance had increased and I hadn't known. The discomfort of my wearing out shoes had not registered and the lack of support had not occurred to me. The unhelpfulness of my gradually wearing out shoes had crept up on me and it had combined with my increasing tolerance and made walking harder for me, yet this had all happened outside of my awareness.

You might say that my old shoes had moulded to the shape of my feet and that they had become more comfortable actually and that the initial breaking in of my new shoes caused quite a bit of pain and made the idea of my old shoes quite appealing. True to an extent, although, once I had got through the brief phase of becoming accustomed to my new shoes the benefits were far greater than the idea of still wearing the old pair. Also, I had to tolerate the initial short-term discomfort of breaking the news shoes in to gain the long-term benefit from them.

Enduring and tolerating things that are not good for us can have roots in many differing areas of who we are. It can come from a lack of self-worth (I put up with this as I'm not worthy) or lowered expectations of what we think is acceptable for us to accept. Others may feel they do or don't deserve this, that or the other. The fear of upsetting the apple cart or in some instances fear that the new shoes, the new car or a new life may be harder to deal with than the worn out and oil filled breaking down situation that they are already in. Also there can be a complete reluctance to consider, contemplate and confront moving on and in some cases literally moving out.

I'm sure that the point I'm making in these examples is obvious, people can go on pouring more oil into the engine of their car whilst walking around in shoes that are wearing out all the while flummoxed as to why things seem to be getting harder. I have seen this type of situation literally thousands of times, where people go on and on and eventually run out of power, become too full of oil or just can't walk any further in worn out shoes. What is behind this? Well, no doubt, tolerance becomes part of the problem, although, so can our lack of awareness.

Of all the qualities, virtues and attributes that people may try to develop, nurture and build up within themselves, such as patience, compassion and generosity, I have found it very rare for people to have self-awareness on this list. Rather people seem more eager to participate in things that will reduce their awareness, make them less receptive and disconnected to what is actually happening to them.

What is really meant by awareness though? Well in very basic terms, being awake, being in touch with what we are experiencing, being tuned in to how we are being affected by the things that are going on around us. Being aware means being switched on, being mindful of our reactions and responses to events, feelings and thoughts. If this doesn't make sense try thinking of the opposite of awareness, as in switched off, dulled down, non-responsive, not really there and then flip that on its head. Imagine what you would be able to sense if you had a huge heavy black tarpaulin thrown over you engulfing you completely. Increasing your self-awareness would be the equivalent of crawling out from underneath it.

There is a terrific poem that nicely sums this up about the person who falls into the same deep hole in the pavement every time they walk down the street. The hole is very deep and each time it takes longer and longer for them to get out and they get increasingly cross with themselves each time. Eventually, there's a change, they walk down the road once more, see the hole, walk round it and avoid falling in. What changed? Well they have become aware, they realised what has been happening and as a result they have been able to change it. Unfortunately, people can go on falling into holes for very long periods of time without realising that this is happening.

If you are in a position where you are unhappy with how things are for you or if you are struggling with any emotional upset, low mood or distressing feelings an increase in your awareness will contribute significantly to progressing and generally feeling better. It is extremely common for people to suspect that something is going on for them although they don't know what that is exactly.

Meanwhile, further mileage in the oil heavy car and old

shoes chips in very nicely here and increased tolerance of pain and discomfort leads to further and further tolerance.

A further example of a lack of awareness is how thousands of people have told me that they worry, all of the time.

Ok, I may reply, *"What do you worry about?"*

The most common answer is, *"everything"*.

"Wow, this must be completely awful" might be my response.

I enquire a little further.

"Do you worry about the battery in your kitchen clock running out?"

Of course the answer to this may be yes although I would hedge my bets that the answer would be no.

When I then intentionally ask about quite randomised and unusual elements of life people find that their claim of worrying about "everything, all the time" is not true.

I might further ask:

"Do you worry about the precision of the time on your watch?"

"Do you worry about somebody stealing your mail?"

Mostly, people answer these questions with a no.

So, this is another example of how it is possible for our lack of awareness to be our enemy as we become so switched off and de-tuned from what is truly happening to us. As a result we get to the point where we sincerely feel that we worry about "everything, all the time".

Worrying all the time, about everything, every single minute, every single day about absolutely everything is something that obviously seems unlikely, although, I have heard this sort of statement not just hundreds but thousands of times, maybe it sounds familiar to you?

I mention this type of situation as I hope it is a relatable example of such reduced awareness where people sincerely feel that their worries are about everything and that they are relentless.

Dulled off awareness can and does easily lead to global generalised statements such as "all the time" and "everything". Global statements and generalisations lead to poor perspective, which leads to unhelpful thinking, which leads to low mood, which leads to further tolerance, which leads to further reduction in awareness, which leads to....

In such an instance as this, the first step would be for that person to actually look at, write down and record when they truly do worry, where are they, what is happening to them, who are they with, what were they feeling like and what were they doing. Once a person's awareness increases the light bulbs rapidly go on and people begin to see things more clearly, with more awareness, and guess what, they feel better.

But how do you become a more fully paid up member of the wide-awake club? Firstly, take off the blinkers that are suppressing your view and remove the goggles that are restricting your potential to experience more, live more fully and understand yourself more. How? Well, literally envisage yourself actually doing that, what would you be able to sense and take in if you removed the sunglasses that are blocking out things of beauty and inspiration. Really, imagine in your minds eye throwing away the pair of glasses that restrict your ability to be you. If you feel that you have also tolerated too much just imagine how things will be if you can remove the shades that have gradually blurred your vision. Do it, throw them away, you don't need them. The sun may blind you to begin with, but after a short while you will feel it's warmth on your face and as that happens I hope you stamp on your suppressive sunglasses.

Secondly, just slow down and yes, it can be that simple! Slipping into automatic rhythms, default speeds and paces that things usually get carried out at, is emotionally fatal. I am quite fanatical about this and I completely refuse to adopt the speeds and tempos that others seem to fall into, without them realising, without their awareness.

Whether I am in the supermarket pushing the trolley around, or in traffic or in conversation, I make a concerted, conscious effort not to allow myself to lapse into the speed and pace that others are going at. There is an interesting musical, for want of a better word, "trick" that you can carry out, you can ask a group of people to simply start clapping without giving them any indication of the speed you want them to clap at. I can guarantee you that in less than five seconds they will all be clapping at exactly the same synchronised speed. Whether it be a safety in numbers response or directed by a fear of not wanting to stand out, I don't know, but I do know that slipping into the rhythms, patterns and speeds that everybody else automatically adopts will definitely reduce your awareness and as a result reduce your ability to think clearly, think independently and make choices that are truly yours.

So, take a second or two and just check yourself and then ask yourself are you about to talk, walk, think, eat, write or move at a speed that is not one you would actually choose?

Are you just allowing yourself to be swept up in the slipstream of life? Take a second to disconnect from the hamster wheel that so many people seem to gladly jump into. You won't lose any key time, you will actually be more productive, make smarter decisions and enjoy a significant boost in awareness. You might even find you are chuckling under your breath as you see others dashing around wasting immense amounts of energy, tolerating this and all the while becoming less and less aware that this is happening right before their eyes. So, slower, avoid automatic speeds and slipping into the pace of others, set your own tempo, take charge of what you allow to happen to you. Awareness is essential, be in charge of boosting yours.

Thirdly, make time. I guess this might be extremely controversial of me to suggest this bearing in mind the frantic nature of the world these days, but, yes, seriously, make time. I'm not talking heaps of time, I'm just talking 10 minutes each day. Go somewhere alone, somewhere quiet, no music, no "stuff" and just sit and just be, just be you. You will find that within a few moments the clutter of the day and the hectic schedule that you might be dealing with will drift away. In this time, don't do anything, just sit and let your thoughts go wherever they want to, just focus on the idea of simply being. Give yourself 10-15 minutes that's all, I am certain you will find that positive and uplifting thoughts will occur, even if they don't and you find that unpleasant thoughts and experiences pop into your mind, persevere with this. Just a few minutes at least two or three times per week will really set you in good stead and refresh your mind and reset your emotional perspective. If you want to further enhance this you could close your eyes and imagine waves of tension and disturbance that might have become clung to you draining away. I do this purposefully, I intentionally try to sense emotional junk leaving me. I just breathe in and let the friction that has somehow gotten its claws into me drift away. I imagine the friction that has built up in me disappearing like waves. This works, but you need to try and you do need to practise this. It will be worth it, I am sure that just a few attempts at this will really hold major benefits for you. After all, what strategies are you using at the moment? So, give this a whirl, be positive about the benefits of it. You need to become you and you will always struggle to achieve this whilst you are subconsciously immersed in the world's devious methods to control you, dull you down and steal your awareness - stealing your awareness to use it against you for unscrupulous reasons which are disguised as being good and beneficial to you.

Just imagine walking around wearing a blindfold. You would feel lost and out of control, you would be constantly bumping into things, you would hurt yourself, you would become more and more frustrated and angry that things were happening to you that you didn't want to. You would eventually drop to your knees, worn out by not being able to see what was happening to you. This is a metaphor that can resemble how people may attempt to go through life, blindfolded, confused and getting more and more hurt and angry. I would encourage you greatly to throw away any blindfold, or any barrier that is blocking your awareness or hampering you from taking in your life, your world and your future.

The psychiatrist, Milton Erickson, intentionally used quite unusual techniques with his patients. For example, he recommended dancing lessons to a couple who were experiencing marital issues. He felt that this would increase their levels of co-operation and communication and that they would find new ways to work together, perhaps even find this enjoyable.

A man who was suffering very badly from depression and felt he could not go on like this any longer visited Erickson. At this time Erickson's clinic was in Vienna with all its beautiful architecture and scenery. He told the man that he wanted him to walk around Vienna and count all the spires on the churches, to observe the churches in detail and to write down all he saw and come back to see him in a week and that this was the end of the appointment. The man was quite aghast at this and was angry and confused at Erickson's apparent lack of help. However, he did indeed follow the instructions he was given and returned to Erickson's clinic one week later a very transformed man. He was gushing about the stunning sites that he had seen and what an amazing place Vienna was and that his mood had been significantly better.

So, what happened here? Well, the depressed man had walked around with his head down, looking at the ground, being inwardly focused and not engaged with the outside world and most importantly unaware that this was happening, unaware of his surroundings and unaware of how he was allowing this to continually lower his mood. Erickson's intervention required the man to look up, to look around and take in his surroundings, to become more aware of all the things that he was missing and to wake up to the beauty of his environment and to be amazed by it. Awareness of both the external and internal is essential and it is imperative that you increase both to enable you move on and feel better.

I have intentionally written about awareness at the start of this book although in a series of therapy sessions it usually comes up somewhere after session four. It usually gets established that unhelpful thinking styles are being used although, as previously mentioned, people aren't sure exactly what they are or when they happen. At this point it is usually appropriate to discuss awareness. This has to be the sequence as it's not possible to for people to try to become aware if they don't know what it is they are trying to become more aware of. But so that you are able to make the most of the forthcoming chapters we are doing things almost in reverse, by talking about awareness first so that you can maximise the advice that I hope you find here.

Your awareness is your true secret weapon, use it to your advantage, increase it, nurture it and feel empowered!

Essential points to remember from Chapter One

- Putting too much oil in your car?
- Are you about to have a leak?
- Are you stumbling around in worn out shoes?
- Remember there is a <u>downside </u>of tolerance.
- Are you aware of what is happening?
- Are you making unhelpful global statements?
- Ditch your suppressive sunglasses.
- Slow down, don't fall into automatic speeds.
- Make time to just, be.

Chapter Two

So, what is wrong with me?

"One of the toughest duties I have from time to time is to break it to people that, despite what they may wish to believe, actually they do not sport an S on their chest, they are not Superman, woman, girl or boy. In my experience...."

Chapter Two
So, what is wrong with me?

People access therapy for many reasons, sometimes it's due to hitting a brick wall, sometimes it's due to an accident that they have been involved in, sometimes they are fed up of feeling as they do, sometimes people have gotten so low or anxious that they can't carry on. It is extremely common, though, for people to seek help when things have become almost unbearable. This can sometimes lead to the early days of the therapy being taken up with enabling that person to work through and settle their basic emotions to arrive at a point where we can really get to work with the goals and aims of the therapy.

Alongside this, quite often, people have endured things for a long time (often decades) and if unhelpful behaviours have become very ingrained and embedded it might also lead to a slow start. This is fine, of course, but it can create a speed bump at the start of the sessions. For some, being part of a therapeutic process or experience can often feel surreal, odd and even a little weird to begin with and sometimes people need time to adapt to the idea of meeting with a virtual stranger and talking about themselves and confronting things that have been avoided for a very long time in some cases.

However, despite these occasional, initial barriers momentum can soon build and people can feel empowered and more able to address things and get to where they want to be. Yet, somewhere along the line, this good progress is often hindered by the question "So, Ian, tell me, what is it that is actually wrong with me?" This question is frequently posed to me in a "this will be our little secret" style, yet almost always, my response to this is, "Nothing, there is nothing *wrong* with you at all". However, my answer is very rarely accepted, even if I offer many very solid examples of what that person has been through, what they have endured, how they have actually been quite heroic and battled through so much to still be here. Even more so, how they are being responsible and mature by working with somebody like me, trying to address what it is that they are dealing with.

Sometimes this kind of situation can become a little bizarre with certain people who have truly suffered so much, yet still contest that the fact they have come to see a therapist and aren't breezing through life surely must indicate that they are incapable of coping or dealing with things and the aforementioned classic "everybody else seems to be ok" followed by the timeless chestnut "there is always somebody else worse off" fill the air. Maybe there are instances where that could be true, yet I feel it is such a pointless point as where do you draw the line with it? Does the person with one arm compare themselves to the person with no arms, who compares themselves to the person with no arms and only one leg, who compares themselves to the person with no.......you get the idea.

Just to be a little more specific on that point, I'm talking about people who, for example, have suffered multiple family deaths in very short periods of times (less than a year) who are furious with themselves simply because they feel like they want to cry. People who, for example, have seen dreadful atrocities in war zones confused by the fact that they "always feel like I am gonna snap". People who have been treated truly dreadfully by colleagues, "friends" or partners, who then go on to badly berate themselves because they feel that they just can't answer the phone or go out. These examples are closely followed by people who feel relentlessly compelled to do things to Olympic gold medal standards who then feel rigid with guilt when they can't keep this up despite extraordinary herculean efforts to do so. Also, the person who has allowed vast levels of resentment, frustration and anger to build up so much that it feels as though they will explode at the tiniest provocation, yet, they are terrified of this happening as they would be mortified if they hurt anybody's feelings (their own don't count you see).

One of the toughest duties I have from time to time is to break it to people that despite what they may wish to believe actually they do not sport an S on their chest, they are not Superman, woman, girl or boy. In my experience this is rarely received with relief and a healthy refreshing of perspective, it is more frequently met with disappointment. The news that we are human, very fragile at times and that virtually everybody is affected at some point in their life often does not comfort people. Sometimes it causes more disappointment towards self, more irritation that seemingly they weren't good enough, people can so badly lack self-compassion at times. Please know that I understand this empathically and I know fully that no one wants to fall short of standards they want to achieve, yet such endeavours, methods, beliefs and approaches so often lead to everything but the long term accomplishment of life's aims, goals and dreams. Returning to my point, so many, many times I see people become really stuck in this search of trying to fathom out what is "wrong" with them. I can find that I am constantly battling with some patients who are almost hell bent on trying to convince me that they truly are faulty or dodgy in some way and that they are somehow innately inferior or flawed. I have, many times, been party to the equivalent of a top level sales pitch as I have listened to people's quite compelling efforts to persuade me that I am either wrong, have missed something or that I might not quite be able to see or tell that they really are weird, messed up, nutty or not quite as complete as the next person!

In therapy, this is usually referred to as "pathologising", the activity where people become quite fixated that not only are they substandard but that they themselves actually are "the problem". I'm not talking about people feeling that they contribute to things being problematic or that in some way they keep the problem going (which happens in nearly every case) no, it's that people literally feel that they themselves are "the problem".

I am going to resist excessively looking at what might lie behind this and delving into a deep and convoluted mystery when maybe it's not really needed. What is more important than where this comes from is what's keeping it going. Well, it might not be breaking news or rocket science to declare that arguing the case that you are the problem is linked with poor self-esteem, low self-worth and not valuing who we are. It's also based in blame though and dropping into a habit of just looking at oneself and assuming that it has to be me, feeling that I must be the person who has caused this and as I mentioned before, seemingly looking around at others and assuming that they are all ok and that they are managing easily and with no problems.

How does self-blame come about? Well, a lack of empowerment throughout the years, an absence of nurturing in childhood, abusive relationships, allowing others to pass the buck, unrealistic expectations and prolonged periods of self-doubt are all very common factors.

Once this self-blame sets in it usually results with highly inaccurate cognitive conclusions such as "I'm not in control of what's going on", "I'm not dealing with things", "I'm not capable and I can't cope" and many, many other uber detrimental statements. This then gets glued onto a nice side order of further self-doubt, complemented by a serving of guilt and a growing tendency to tap into "proof" to back this up and hey presto people become convinced that there is something wrong with them.

Of course, this isn't the one and only way that people can fall into looking at themselves as the problem, although it is a pattern that I have seen many thousands of times. Then this usually results in becoming embroiled in maintaining this self-imposed, highly negative identity. As in most emotional struggles, once a person arrives at a conclusion or definition of who they feel they are i.e. worthless, useless, pathetic, they usually turn confirming this impression of themselves into a lifelong endeavour. This often involves confirming far more negatives than positives and taking on board inaccurate information from inaccurate sources and detuning from our own intuitive sense of what is good, bad, right, wrong, helpful or unhelpful. It also commonly involves wasting precious energy, time and effort, which ends up with people feeling tired and lethargic, no prizes for figuring out what this does to a person's ability to think.

So, instances of reinforcing a negative view of who we might think we are can range from forgetting car keys to going for an inappropriate job interview to virtually anything that will further confirm a blossoming sense of being incompetent in some way. Once this perspective becomes rigid and fixed it just becomes the norm and a little bit like the furniture in your rooms that hasn't been moved around for a long time and when it finally comes to considering rearranging things it can get uncomfortable. Then the case for keeping the old, worn out and unhelpful actually gets strengthened. The resistance to look at ourselves in a more compassionate, positive light can take quite a battering before anything remotely optimistic, self-boosting or uplifting gets through.

In these instances I frequently compare a person's thoughts, perspective and attitude, particularly towards themselves, to a scaffolding framework that has become rusty, locked in place and unmoved for such a long time. Then along comes the therapy that tries to clamber on top of this framework and to rock it, shake it, dislodge the parts that have become jammed and stuck. The residents will obviously protest and complain that it is too frightening, (will the old scaffolding poles be strong enough, can they be mended) despite experiencing a sense that it could be better and much more beneficial in the long run.

People's insistence in searching for further reasons to blame themselves and to assess what is wrong rather than right with them and seeking further insight into the negative rather than the positive can become quite embedded, almost like a way of life. The reluctance and resistance to change, yet claiming to be tired and worn out from living life in unhelpful ways, is clung to and when it comes down to it the path well walked on, the familiar and the common once again hold appeal.

So, what's going on? Could this all be connected with a fear of being truly liberated, set free and empowered? It was Soren Kierkegaard who said that we can take up all of our freedom saying we have no freedom. If people are given the keys to the kingdom, given the access code for the cell door and the combination that will open the padlock, does this become more daunting than the prospect of remaining unhappy, depressed and anxious? It is one of the most common clichés in the world that people don't like change, true enough I guess, yet what I feel I am talking about here is more akin to allowing ourselves to suffer. Suffer with inaccurate perceptions of who we are, suffer by feeding ourselves inaccurate information and suffer by blaming ourselves over and over again.

Is this also connected with the fear of giving ourselves the permission to be fantastic, fabulous and fearless? I suspect it might be, as I mentioned, tolerance can be an enemy.

I have, with my own eyes, seen people go through a virtual living hell even while the opportunity to escape was in touching distance.

So, in an effort to avoid freedom and liberation perhaps the safest bet of ensuring further torture and slavery is to look at oneself and hijack the possibility of freedom by asking "So, what is wrong with me?" "What you say makes sense, I can see how I will feel better and I get what you are saying, but tell me, what actually is my problem?"

It is as though people actually want a dreadful diagnosis, something that they can perhaps latch onto as a basis for their identity, something that might give them justification for what they are experiencing, as often, simple reassurances such as how they are is to be expected, understandable and "normal" don't seem to cut it. In other words it is almost as though people are saying, can't I be locked up for a little longer, can't you help me search for more reasons to feel bad about myself, instead of helping me, can't you really do something for me and contribute to keeping me stuck. Sometimes it is as though people want me, as a therapist, to further condemn them and make their suspicions official somehow by giving them the rubber stamp, which states that they are doomed. Of course not everybody is like this, yet, in my experience, I have found that it is very common at some level, whether it be completely consigning themselves to the scrap yard, or allowing some kind of limitation on ability or competence to dominate them. Also tapping into beliefs that, their body, their intelligence, their stamina is not quite up to the job and some form of self-imposed restriction also usually puts in an appearance somewhere along the line.

We recently adopted three fantailed Goldfish, which are such beautiful creatures. We were also given the 35 litre tank to keep them in, this was an orb shaped tank which we soon realised was quite cramped for them. We were told again and again that Goldfish grow to the size of their environment and if we bought a bigger tank they would flourish and grow to the size of it, a 125 litre tank was recommended which was more than double their current space! I hope you can see my point, are you allowing yourself to live in too small a fish tank? Are you living in a cramped emotional world, do you need to exist where there is more mental space for you to grow?

In Alice in Wonderland, Alice asks "How does one become a butterfly?" the reply is "You must want to fly so much that you are willing to give up being a Caterpillar".

So, does this apply to you? Do you blame yourself? Do

you have a "cap in hand" mentality when it comes to moving on? Might you have developed a habit of boosting your apparent shortcomings, might you have become more skillful at promoting your "weaknesses" instead of your strengths, might you have become more inclined to do yourself down instead of boosting yourself up? Have you come to prefer the prison cell instead of the open road?

If so, what is it going to be? When you stand once again at the T-junction, which way will you turn? Will you lean once again on your old frenemie tolerance and go through even more suffering and trudge once again down the road marked familiar, yet painful and likely to lead to more misery? Or will you choose the road marked new, scary, hopeful and potentially magical?

Will you let yourself, once again, unnecessarily go through distress, doubt and depression? I hope you will choose wisely.

Essential points to remember from Chapter Two

- Are you trying to be Superhuman?
- Are you looking for something to be wrong with you?
- Do you blame yourself when there is no justification?
- Are you reinforcing a negative view of yourself?
- Do you lack compassion for yourself?
- Are you afraid of freedom?
- Are you living in a fish tank that is too small?
- Are you ready to give up on being a caterpillar?

Chapter Three

The K.I.S.S. Theory

"Trapping ourselves by buying into our own con trick that we know what is about to happen, when and where and involving whom……."

Chapter Three
The K.I.S.S. Theory

In my former life (as I refer to it) I was lucky enough to fulfill my childhood ambition of being a musician. From being about eight years old I was completely consumed by the desire to work in bands and groups and to be a performer on stage. My sisters who would play records in our "front room" inspired me and my urge to work in music thrived. I was a walking musical encyclopedia and I practiced and practiced as soon as I got home from school. I would literally throw down my school bag and go immediately to my keyboard and play and play. I still laugh now as I remember how my Dad used to call my first ever synthesizer *"that bloody Hurdy Gurdy!"*

I worked as a pianist full time for nearly 23 years and I began writing songs with Chris in 2003. To say we hit it off is an understatement and to make a long story short we came across Randy Stalls in 2006. Randy is a very successful and highly effective promoter and music producer based in North Carolina. I first spoke with Randy in a three-way conference call early in 2006, where, to be honest, he scared the living daylights out of me! He proclaimed that I needed to get on a plane and *"Come to America and record your music with me!"* He further stated that if I didn't do this I would one day wake up an old man and I would look for the biggest rock I could find and that I would beat myself on the head with it until I had no brains left! *"So, come to America my brother Ian!"*

We did indeed fly to North Carolina to work with Randy and the trip did go very well and we did have some amazing success from this. We had been there though for three days when Randy asked us if we knew *"the K.I.S.S. theory"*? We shook out heads quite ignorantly to which he replied *"Huh, I thought you English guys knew everythang"*.

The K.I.S.S. theory, forgive me if you already know this, stands for Keep It Simple Stupid. I made a conscious decision to include the theory in this book aware that some people may already be familiar with it, although, I hope my perspective on it and the points that I will make might give you further insight and an enhanced view on it. If you have not previously heard of the K.I.S.S. theory then you are about to!

How does this all connect with the themes of this book and my work as a psychotherapist? Well, one of the most common and most disabling activities that I see is extremely high levels of over thinking. I see people spend hours and hours wasting precious time, energy, effort and love poring over things that don't matter, things that are so unlikely to happen, linking things together that have no real connection at all and creating such high levels of tension, dread and concern. I also have been told, by literally thousands of people, that they know they are doing this and they know that when they fall into this trap they struggle and find life harder. Also, that their mood dramatically lowers as does their energy, motivation, general interest in life, hobbies and being around others.

There are five frogs on a log, one of them thinks about jumping in, how many frogs are left on the log? Five. Because he only thought about jumping in!

One of the key problems with over thinking, speculating and ruminating on things is, as the old saying goes, it leads a person to spend too much time in their own heads. This occurs at the expense of gathering new experiences that would give new insight, new information and a new basis that would go on to influence how things can develop. As you can see that the frog only thought about jumping off the log. Ok, so yes, it's true that new experiences could go badly and might lead to worse thinking, I would say to you though that even new, real, unhappy or unhelpful experiences are better than allowing ever increasing junk to gradually thrive in your head as you give it more airtime and attention. Any real experience will contain some kind of learning, some kind of benefit, how many times do children fall over and get up again when they are learning to walk? They learn to walk by getting up over and over again, not by extreme lengths of scrutiny as to why they fell, what or who caused it and what might the consequences be if they were to fall again.

Over thinking is often accompanied by gazing into the crystal ball. The old faithful crystal ball, which people tend to glare into far too often for their own good. Crystal balls come in all shapes and sizes and some can even be conveniently kept in people's pockets or handbags so that they can be whipped out at a seconds notice. The findings of the crystal ball are often the basis for decisions, beliefs, actions, thoughts and behaviours. Just as a mystic would, people look into their own crystal balls and allow themselves to predict all kinds of dread, doubt and doom over their futures.

You could also call this fortune telling, where people feel that they can extremely accurately predict what is about to happen. Whether it is that they are going to have a panic attack, or that they will lose control of their bowels, they will die if their heart rate goes too fast, others will negatively talk about them if they go out socially, they will be ostracised if they speak their minds and the list goes on. It can so often be the case that people base an immense amount of their actions, thoughts and behaviours on their insistence in their ability to gaze into their crystal ball and fortune tell the future.

Part of the reason that this belief in mystical ability increases, is that once a person becomes anxious, uptight or fearful their senses become heightened. This is meant to happen when there is genuine threat, yet people can trigger this off without any real need. Heightened seeing, hearing and feeling can pick up on all kinds of things that a settled, balanced and calm individual doesn't. For example, a "niggle" in my chest, the apparently broken CCTV camera, the potential shortcomings of the doctor and medical equipment etc, etc, etc. Following this, usually, there is an increased sense of faith in this flourishing mystical "ability". An "I told you so" mentality grows and people allow the findings of this heightened state to resemble reality, allow it to be believable and this gets thrown into the melting pot of ever growing doubt and fear. The crystal ball gladly reinforces the uncertainty and sadly the show goes on.

Of course, fortune telling is just not possible, not for me, not for you or any mystic or prophet who tries to convince us that it is. Fortune telling either combined with or as a sister of excessive over thinking is part and parcel of speeding down the emotional road to ruin. Trapping ourselves by buying into our own con trick that we know what is about to happen, when and where and involving whom is a sure fire way to remain anxious, unsure and uncertain. If you do wish to remain a prisoner, to what is referred to as anxiety, I can guarantee you that you will achieve this by increasing the level of uncertainty that you experience by believing too much in your capability to fortune tell the future.

Over-thinking also can lead to a self-made cynicism and a self-held conviction that "I am right". Excessive time spent poring over absolutely anything under the sun can lead people to create convincing cases that their fears, concerns and issues are increasingly likely to happen and also that everybody else can't see this. Over-thinking is the opposite of over-experiencing, it is the opposite of over-reality and the opposite of over-authenticity. Over-thinking can make the un-imaginable seem possible, the distinct seem inevitable and turn the far reached into the seemingly unavoidable. If you don't believe me, try it out, intentionally spend all day brooding over something that is bothering you to a scale of say 5-10. Por over it all day, non-stop, look for answers and solutions and see the effect that it has on you.

There is the quite quaint expression that I like which goes "analysis, paralysis" which sums things up very succinctly. The immense potential that we all have in our minds is so often wasted on things that can ensure we stay stuck, or even worse, start to go in reverse when we sink into unhelpful scrutiny that increasingly examines the detail of the detail. Vigorously looking for threat in the tiniest aspect of life that so often just does not exist or is less likely to happen than winning the lottery! This further reinforces our fears, doubts and increases the sense that something awful will happen. So why would you do it?

When it comes to finding ways to deal with this, it can be tempting to get involved with intricate strategies and begin to make dealing with over-thinking a further exercise in excessive thinking! This also then becomes a more intellectual occurrence rather than an emotional one, moving you further away from your own inbuilt intuitive sense of what you might want to do, when and why. I would strenuously encourage you to avoid over-thinking at all costs, for the reasons I have mentioned and many more besides.

So, how is this best achieved? I feel this doesn't need to be any more complicated than remembering Randy and the K.I.S.S. theory. Please do not dismiss the K.I.S.S. theory as ineffective because of it's simplicity, it is this simplicity that is it's real strength and effectiveness. I use this to great effect in many areas of my life, from what will I have for breakfast, to which project I may work on next, to what I will do at the weekends. Please do not allow yourself to lapse into such unhelpful excessive energy zapping analysis on people, places and things, leaving you not knowing which way to turn other than retreating to a further ongoing fearful emotional state.

Use a more simplistic approach, get rid of the internal discussions and ditch the endless to-ing and fro-ing that will get you nowhere. Throw away your crystal ball and replace it with regular dose of reality, tap into your senses and truly experience what happens when you take things as they come and allow yourself to increase a much more accurate growing inner faith in your ability, strength and power.

Get real experiences, real reality and real life into your mind and a mental database that will truly allow you to move on rather than strengthening the emotional prison that over-thinking will gladly continue to build for you.

Essential points to remember from Chapter Three

- Get new actual experiences.
- Ditch your crystal ball.
- Are you aware of over thinking? (See Chapter One)
- The K.I.S.S. Theory.
- Practice simplicity.
- Get out there and not in your head.

Chapter Four

The Rule Book

"More frightening than this, though, is the automatic, often unconscious, compliance to the rules in the book......"

Chapter Four
The Rule Book

My five-year-old niece Beatrice is more beautiful than you could imagine, she is just magical, and so special to me. She oozes personality and charm and she is beyond adorable and I love her so dearly.

When she was around three years old she came, one day, to visit our new house and as with most children of that age she was completely inquisitive about it and wanted to explore. So, up the stairs we were about to go when suddenly Beatrice declares:

"Shoes off"

"No, it's ok Beatrice, you can keep them on" I tell her.

Beatrice chimes in again more insistently *"Shoes off"*

"No, no, it's ok you can keep them on" I say.

"Shoes off!"

"No problem Beatrice, really, you can keep them on".

At this point she becomes really animated, upset and begins to cry.

"Shoes off!!"

I agreed. Ok. Shoes off. She stopped crying.

This was a very moving experience and despite how it may seem a little inconsequential, I saw that Beatrice already had highly fixed and highly threatening rules in her mind. There was no way she would have walked upstairs with her shoes on. This was an unbreakable rule, a rule that she felt held severe consequences and one that was totally inflexible. She was unable to hear any alternative suggestion or tune into forms of reassurance. The rule was King. No, actually, it wasn't. The Rule Book was.

So, look, I know I am talking about a three-year child yet I do this intentionally. This is to highlight how "The Rule Book" starts when we are very young and also to highlight how the threat and dreaded consequences of disobeying the rules can apply not just to a three year old but to us all, yes, including me.

Maybe you haven't previously thought about this idea of a rule book and maybe this is a brand new concept to you. If so, well I have news for you, it is likely that a rule book is alive and well within you and also quite likely that it is thriving and that you are nurturing it in one way or another.

One definition of a rule is "a statement that tells you what is or is not allowed" this sums up the key issue that the rule book creates for us, what is or is not, "allowed". Of course, in life there are indeed things that can be referred to as rules which really do need to be observed such as speed limits, don't drink and drive, don't steal, do pay your taxes etc. The rules that I am really talking about here are the more emotionally self-imposed rules and the limiting regulations that create a psychological prison that, ironically, people then bizarrely protest about and seek help to break free from. Rules such as, things have to be perfect, I am not allowed to bother people, my problems are mine to deal with, I am not allowed to get things wrong, I must be in control of things, I cannot show emotion as I will appear vulnerable and so on.

The rule book is often self-authored as we go through life, although, it usually features some outstanding contributions from parents, teachers, family, colleagues, partners, friends and others. Often the content of the rule book is deeply disguised as being good for us and keeping us on the right track, ensuring we don't stray, break any "rules", get mixed up with the wrong crowd or un-conform to the seemingly accepted, common and traditional.

However, almost always, the rules that are transmitted our way are borne out of somebody else's fears, doubts and insecurities or are extracts taken from their own rule book and generously donated our way again, usually justified as being good for us. There are common rules that seem to occur in most people's book and they are almost always restrictive and prohibitive in some way, rarely are the rules in the rule book designed to empower us or to truly make life easier. It may appear on the surface of things that they are there to help us, yet on a deeper level, this is not really the case. You see the thing is that rules are inflexible, the old expression goes that you can bend the rules although that's really not the case either. This is the main problem with rules, they are black and white, either you stick to the rule or you break it, there is nothing in between, either you are right or you are wrong, either you are good or you are bad, you are in or you are out, 100% or zero. Guess how this then impacts on our emotions, thoughts and actions, going through life with the threat of either being completely right or completely wrong. Trying to exist within the minimum of give for being human is of course anxiety provoking, stressful and negatively contagious. It is just like giving ourselves a tightrope to walk on, yet, more often than not, there is no safety net, there is no one to catch us when we break the rules. All that does seem to exist at this point, where the rule has inevitably been broken, is that the judge and jury who reside in our headspace begin to berate us for falling off the tightrope and for not being able to keep up with the plethora of rules. Finger wagging at us and questioning why this happened and forging ahead with the inquiry into what went wrong and what is going to occur as a result. An inquiry that we are obligated to attend and where we have to give an account of the truly awful thing known as "lessons learned".

The greek philosopher, Plato, spoke of how those who used to live in caves were exposed to certain images and sounds, which contributed to the shaping of their thoughts and beliefs. However, the cave dwellers did not realise that the images they were observing were actually only their own shadows that were being reflected onto the walls of the cave by the fires they kept. They then began to connect sounds and other images to these shadows and they became real to the cave dwellers and they began to interact with them as such. Yet, if one person were to brave enough to consider leaving the cave, they would then realise the truth about the shadows, they would find out where they were coming from and let go of the fears, thoughts and ideas that they had built up based on the shadows.

Although the sole brave enlightened cave dweller who left the cave and discovered the truth about the shadows now begins to think and act differently he also realises that the perceptions of the other cave dwellers are completely inaccurate. Yet he now fears that if he did decide to share his new knowledge and understanding on what is real, well, the other cave dwellers may ridicule, shun and mock him and more so this may lead them to choosing to further embrace their familiar way of viewing reality. The remaining cave dwellers continue to stay trapped by their favoured ways of thinking and are unable to break away from the patterns of their own thoughts and the enlightened now becomes alienated, unsure of what to do with his new knowledge.

This hopefully highlights how there can be a scary acceptance of self-imposed rules and fears (even when we have no idea where they are coming from) and an adherence to completely unhelpful do's and don'ts and a conformity to them, even when it is clear that they simply do not do us any favours at all. More frightening than this though is the automatic, often unconscious, compliance to the rules in the book.

People come to see me, perhaps brave enough to take a peek out of the cave yet clutching on to what they feel they know. Often though, they are ground down, unable to take much more, with no understanding of how their tolerance of so many debilitating rules has turned them from a free spirit into a slave. A slave more often than not of their own design, influenced by the doubts and worries of others, the dread of what might happen, imaginary shadows on the wall leading to the eventual dulling down of ones senses.

The enemy of tolerance yet again hinders us and leaves us seemingly powerless to change things.

Also the rigidness of these rules so often goes without saying, so rarely do people stop and take stock of the emotional straitjackets that they wear which become tighter and tighter leaving people uncomfortable, frustrated and despirited. The fear of challenging the terms and conditions of the rule book is beyond daunting, such is the power that it can hold. There is so often a resistance to encouragement, persuasion or reassurance, to even begin to defy the rule book and such discussion often lands on deaf ears. Meanwhile those who have stepped out of the "cave" are often viewed with doubt and cynicism. Alas, the rules in the book have become life, the ability to question them, let alone defy them, has become muted.

More powerful still than this though is that we can build

up so many rules that we simply can't help but break one, but, when one does get broken then even more rules have to be put in place, for further prevention of course. This kind of thing is especially common and problematic with people with eating disorders where certain foods are not permissible at certain times. Also certain combinations of foods are not allowed and strict regimes of exercise must be adhered to often leading to further self-imposed sanctions and penalties for non-compliance.

Breaking the rules also holds wider problems, after all, who wants to be the one to stand up and publicly destroy their rule book and what would happen if they did? Liberated individuals, rule breakers and freedom fighters have, throughout the years, been labeled as everything from insane to downright dangerous. Holding onto a rule book and diligently adhering to it can lead to benefits socially, many people clutching on to their rule books can hold convincing sway over others and dissuade them from even thinking about erasing a line or two let alone burning the damn thing!

Rule books can even be seen as adding credibility to us, giving kudos, falling nicely into line, swimming graciously with the tide, blindly ticking boxes and serially subscribing to further bondage, thank you very much. If you feel that your rules actually are your enemy and not good for you and that you may do well to throw them away, well, this may initially prove to be a scary thing for you to do. But guess what, it is a very scary thought for thousands of others too and scary thoughts are highly contagious, so, to set yourself free from your own limiting rules, you might find that not only do you have to fight your own fears, you will have to fight the fears of the others too.

So, the consequences of disobeying the rule book can be unthinkable, yet the sinister thing is that compliance with it is unsustainable and total and complete obedience is completely impossible. It is not achievable no matter what, not matter how much effort, focus, discipline, application or commitment is exercised at some point it is in inevitable that a rule will be broken.

After all what else is it there for, what kind of a self-imposed rule book would we have designed if it didn't contain impossible standards and excessive expectations just to ensure that we don't reach too high for ourselves, just to ensure we don't get too ambitious or too lofty an idea of who we are and what we are capable of. So, once again, if you can relate to this, what is it going to be? Are you going to continue to hold onto inaccurately formed thoughts about who you are, how you should live and let yourself be bossed and dictated to about how things ought to be?

Because, if you let them, then, sadly, the rules, will rule.

Essential points to remember from Chapter Four

- Rules are black and white.
- Think guidelines rather than rules.
- Are there shadows on the walls of your life that are not real?
- Are you wearing an emotional straitjacket?
- Do you have so many rules that you can't help but break one?
- Might you one day look back regretfully on a life controlled by rules?

Chapter Five

The Bottle of Pop

"Emotions of all kinds are possibly the strongest sign of our humanity, our frailties and our beautifully vulnerable human condition....."

Chapter Five
The Bottle Of Pop

My very good friend Matt once told me about how he had, in the past, considered becoming a heavy goods lorry driver just as a way to have more career options and a source of further income should he need it. He told me how the application entailed a medical, which of course, he needed to undergo. During the medical it was pointed out to him that he had a lump in the side of his body. Matt was of course oblivious to this, he was asked if he knew it was there, no, did it hurt, no, nothing, had he felt it before, no never. Matt was advised to visit his doctor immediately, which he did. Matt's doctor confirmed that there was indeed quite a sizeable lump in his side and that it was imperative that it was removed immediately. 24 hours later Matt was undergoing surgery to have the lump removed. It was, thankfully, not malignant or dangerous in anyway yet no chances could be taken, it had to come out and it had to come out now!

Matt tells me that this event significantly affected his outlook on life and that he now tries to cherish everything and to make the most of his family, his hobbies and his future.

Are you wondering what this has got to do with anything? Well, as you might have gathered by now, there are certain commonalities that occur when people go through emotional challenges and as a result people, more often than not, will have fairly predictable answers to certain questions.

For example, *"Do you find the mornings to be difficult?"*, *"Can things usually feel better if you are at home?"* and *"Is your confidence quite low at the moment?"* sometimes the answers to these questions are not quite what I expect, although, more often than not the answers are very, very similar.

However, I can almost guarantee the answers that I will get to the following questions:

1. Do you tell many other people about how you are feeling?
2. Do you keep your feelings bottled up? (the switched on of you will now get the title of this chapter)
3. Have you done these things for a long time?
4. If you have, how long have you done this for?

I know you may not need me to tell you this, yet here goes, the typical answers that I usually get to those four questions are:

1. No, never. I just couldn't. I am just too afraid to. I can't let them know.
2. Yes. Permanently. I have to. Nobody would be interested/understand.
3. Yes. Ages.
4. A long time. To which, I ask, if we are talking weeks or months? We are usually talking decades.

Although I have heard these responses many thousands

of times I am always astonished at the capacity that people have (and can develop) to shut down, lock and force down emotions, especially negative emotions and feelings such as frustration, resentment, anger and hurt. I am also further astonished when people tell me that they feel terrible and like a bottle of pop that will explode at any minute. Is there any wonder, I ask, yet as I have already mentioned people still find a little more space from somewhere to tolerate a little more pain.

I know that the people sat opposite me are intelligent enough to realise that this strategy of keeping things locked in is not the greatest plan in the world and also that it is a key contributing factor to the continuation of the way they feel, yet somehow more containment is achieved and more suppression is managed.

The justifications I usually hear for this though, are the ones I mentioned earlier or variations of them. They wouldn't be able to cope if I told them, I just can't hurt their feelings, I would look stupid, I would look weak, they would laugh, they would tell me to just get on with it.

Ok, I can truly accept that these kinds of responses are not the sort of comments that we would welcome every day of the week, yet they are concerns and fears that are usually formed with a considerable contribution from the previously mentioned crystal ball. I also want you to know that I feel whole-heartedly compassionate, empathic and respectful to these kinds of concerns, yet what I do want to be more vocal about is people's apparent mystery of why they feel so crap when often the writing is on the wall. That writing is massive suppression and containment of extremely infectious negative emotions, pain and distress.

Often this is followed by an internal road rage, where people who contain insane amounts of hurt, loss and abuse then become furious with themselves for not being able to deal with or keep a lid on all that they hold in.

They almost implore me to tell them:

"Ian what is wrong with me, everybody else seems to be ok, why can't I get over this, why can't I cope, why can't I just tell myself to just get on with it?".

I may reply *"Well, perhaps all the feelings that you have kept locked inside of you for all this time is part of what you are dealing with and if you could work through them maybe you would sense some relief".*

The answers that I might usually hear from this are along the lines of those I just mentioned and other examples could be:

"I don't know how to" and

"If I do start to work through them I will be completely overwhelmed and I won't be able to stop it".

Those examples are slightly more helpful and workable than the others that I have mentioned because they are not quite as fixed and they imply a premise that could be tested out.

These points where people trap themselves between immense suppression of emotions and a fear of sharing/expressing them is sometimes known as a double bind. The best example I have ever heard of a double bind is this:

Son goes to Father and Father says,

"Come and give your Dad a kiss"

Then he says,

"Don't be so soppy, boys don't kiss their Dads"

Followed by.....

"What's the matter, don't you love your Dad?"

A double bind, or in more common terms, caught between a rock and hard place. A lose-lose situation, and although this example contained two people the boy and his Dad, the double binds that I see people go through is just them, self-imposed, traps of their own emotional architecture.

I know full well that often there has been many, many significant cruel contributions from others to these emotional straitjackets that people can wear and that these contributions can be ongoing and sometimes a key part of the problem that needs to be addressed before anything else can change. Although, at the end of the day, it is ourselves that need to push the button, even if we are aided by much help, love, support, guidance and encouragement, it is our fingers that have to reach out and flick the switch. Flick the switch in our heads, hearts and minds that says things have to change.

Ok, so how does this begin? Well, I feel it begins not by talking about emotionally freeing exercises, buzz words, mantras or affirmations, but it begins with a change in our attitude on how we view locked in negative emotions. Rather that they are not seen as an unavoidable part and parcel of life that have to be endured or things that we must keep as internal prisoners, no, they need to be seen as lethal as a cancer, tumour, shrapnel or the lump that Matt had.

I feel I can safely say that if we were given the news that we did indeed have cancer or a tumour for example we would have no hesitation in getting it removed from our bodies. We would be emphatic in our urgency to get this taken out of our body before it got any worse or caused any further damage or pain. The same would apply for what might be considered of lesser threat, such as infections, splinters or something that might cause indigestion or an upset stomach. These things are viewed with a significantly different perspective to emotions, yet they can be as dangerous. Suppressed negative emotions do not go away, they do not reduce in intensity, they do not decide to up and leave one day thinking that they will do us a favour. Suppressed negative emotions grow and increase in their impact on us and they will have their way with us one day.

You see, our bodies are sealed units with only certain pathways that things are allowed to enter and leave from and our bodies will attempt to repel anything that is a foreign body, a threat or anything that this simply not meant to be there. People who are about to end their lives by assisted suicide need to drink a certain fluid before drinking the actual substance that will end their lives, as that final substance will be repelled by our stomachs, it will recognise the toxic quality of it and it will attempt to eject it from our body. Not meant to be there you see.

The same thing happens with emotions, our minds and bodies sense the danger they pose and we are given messages and instructions, just as with any form of unwelcome visitor they cannot stay. These messages, though, are frequently ignored and not acted upon. People tell me, I feel like I want to scream, it doesn't happen, I feel like I want to run away and cry, it doesn't happen, I feel like I will explode if I don't tell them how I feel, it doesn't happen. What does happen, more often than not, is that these feelings are not given a voice, not given an outlet or given the chance to be expressed and aired, instead they are re-routed and fed back inside where they further paralyse us, they grow and grow in intensity and drain us of energy, focus and motivation. Negative emotions really do need to be seen with the same perspective as a threatening disease or condition, seen as poisonous and dangerous and as something that cannot be allowed to dwell, let alone thrive within us. That is not if we are eager to move on, feel better and do better.

The World Health Organisation suggests that health is a state of complete physical, mental and social wellbeing and not merely the absence of disease or infirmity. Yet, the key here is that you cannot achieve well-being whilst your body has emotional disease or infirmity, our entire emotional balance depends on the absence of repressed feelings, suppressed anger, forced down frustration, restricted resentment and hidden hurt. Imagine trying to smoothly walk and be beautifully balanced with a ball and chain or weights around your feet, it just wouldn't be possible, yet this is the completely fruitless task I see so many people try to take on and attempt to conquer.

So, more than looking at how negative emotions are dealt with, I want to encourage you to change your perspective on them, and see them as the threat they are to you and your wellbeing and that you begin to recognise them to be as sinister as cancers, tumours and infections. Also, please do not underestimate the power of emotions, especially negative emotions, one percent of emotion will defeat a million per cent of logic, attempted rational thinking and what might seem like balanced mental negotiations. Trying to reason with your feelings and emotions with "logic" is only going to lead you to further twist and turn the natural course that your emotions want to take, it's like trying to prevent yourself from vomiting by trying to swallow and swallow it back, mixing logic and emotions is like square pegs and round holes. They don't fit and they never will.

The real objective is to accept that you feel as you do and to allow your feelings to be expressed, voiced and for them to take their course. Also, will your predictions come true, will you be overwhelmed by them, will they laugh, will they think you are stupid? If they do, so what? Is this reality talking to you or your crystal ball? Similarly, people often make matters so much worse by adding tension, negative feelings and negative energy to periods of low mood so rather than giving those feelings an escape route they get cancelled out (well, in the short term they do).

Cancelling out your emotions is tantamount to cancelling out yourself, it is akin to saying that as my feelings don't matter so neither do I and why would you do that if you do truly want to move on?

Emotions of all kinds are possibly the strongest sign of our humanity, our frailties and our beautifully vulnerable human condition and maybe it is because of this that some people dislike them. Any expressed emotion transforms the person expressing it, expressed emotions can make us look idiotic, I think of myself singing with a look of demented elation at football matches leaping around hugging strangers.

Emotions can make us look fragile and delicate, crying at a sad movie for example and they can make us look triumphant and imperious. They are the surest sign that we are real, we are not icebergs, robots or machines, they indicate that we are not stagnant or static, we are dynamic, alive and interacting with our environments, the people in them and the stimulation we receive, whether we like it or not. We are real and we have strengths, vulnerabilities and frailties, things that, seemingly, don't make sense can affect us and we can feel boosted or deflated, and it is the acceptance to this realness that is the absolute key to emotional wellbeing.

However, excessive and highly dangerous habits and behaviours can be formed to try to combat this realness, such as excessive alcohol consumption, self-harm, using drugs or isolation. Yet sooner or later people who employ these avoidance tactics are often confronted with themselves, their emotions and their realness.

So, I would encourage you to embrace your emotions and see them for what they are, the undeniable, unavoidable evidence that you are alive! This means that you need to strenuously avoid compressing them, especially negative ones as they will catch up with you, have the opposite effect and make you feel as though you are not living, merely contending with life.

Don't allow your emotions to become like a vigorously shaken up bottle of pop that may erupt. You need to ensure also that you manage your feelings regularly. If your bottle of pop is almost always more than eighty percent full and letting out only a little now and then but nothing changes, it's going to get shaken once more and it's not going to take much for it to get fit to bursting all over again. Whereas if your bottle is say 40-50 percent full you have some leeway to give yourself so that you are not living life almost always emotionally maxed out!

Matt's lump, thankfully, was not dangerous, but still it had to come out, negative emotions are dangerous if you do not permit them to be voiced, expressed or allow them to take their course. For anyone not feeling great, suppressed negative emotions will only serve to add further debilitating vibes to what may already be a very difficult situation.

We only have a limited amount of emotional and physical space that we can assign and allocate to emotions in general and negative emotions take up more room than others. This space is expandable and can stretch, if needed, for a while, yet it will then encroach into space and energy usually reserved for other essential elements and this expansion is not a terrific long term plan. You need to allow your emotions to come out to make space for more to come in, like emotional traffic, you need to avoid becoming gridlocked, do all you can to give your emotions breathing space, thinking space and feeling space.

I guess it would be somewhat remiss of me to write a chapter like this and not address how we might go about expressing our emotions. Well, as in previous chapters where, for example, combatting over thinking often becomes an exercise in over thinking itself, expressing our emotions does not need to become an emotionally turbulent time.

Think of what you might do to suppress your emotions and feelings and do the opposite, listen to the messages that you might be ignoring, respond to the vibrancy of being real. Once again, think simple. Emotions are only difficult to express if we let them be, talk to somebody, anybody, write down your feelings (yes, this does really help), put on your favourite movie or music, turn up the music full blast, stamp your feet, cry your eyes out, do these things often and repeatedly, as the old saying goes "Get it out of your system".

The most important thing is not the how you get negative emotions out of your system, no, the essential thing is the why. Establishing an attitude and perspective that understands the importance of not allowing the bottle of pop scenario to occur is the first crucial step, the how will be easy once this is achieved. I reckon that almost everybody could come up with some kind of physical exercise plan without any guidance, so they would have the "how to" knowledge, yet more often than not underlying factors are not accepted for what they are and it is the "why" that stops the how from occurring. So it's not the how you work with your emotions that is the key thing you need to know, it is the why. Don't delay this opportunity to see yourself for who you are, it doesn't have to be a confrontation, let it be the equivalent of hugging a long lost friend.

If somebody told you that they were intentionally, defiantly and consciously going out of their way not to have the progressive life threatening and potentially terminal cancer removed from their body and they were just going to leave it there and do nothing about it, what would you think of them?

There is no difference with negative emotions. I rest my case.

Essential points to remember from Chapter Five

- Are you guilty of suppression?
- Do you put yourself in double binds?
- What is your perspective on negative emotions?
- Emotions mean you are real. Be real!
- Empty your bottle often.
- Not the how but the why.
- Matt's lump.

Chapter Six

Uncertainty

"However, people build up such high levels of dependency on safety behaviours that they wind up generating even higher levels of uncertainty than there were to begin with....."

Chapter Six
Uncertainty

Perhaps you know the old saying that nothing in life is anymore certain than that things will be uncertain. As it goes, uncertainty is not always a topic of conversation that is as common as the weather (unless you're talking about the uncertainty of the weather that is) yet it is an undeniable fact of life, and, as with some other themes in this book, it cannot be eradicated no matter what, never, it is here to stay. No matter how much money, love, intelligence, muscle power, faith or confidence you have you will at some point need to go through uncertainty.

Whether we like it or not uncertainty does surround us all the time, in everything, everyday we live with it, sometimes we are keenly aware of it, whilst at other times we just brush it off. Daily we deal with such intense and frequent levels of uncertainty that might scare the living daylights out of us if we took the time to stop and think about how much uncertainty we actually do endure and how uncertain things actually are.

Uncertainty has this very debilitating effect on us, it impacts on our thoughts, moods and actions. For example, just ask anybody who has recently bought or moved house how the experience affected them and I reckon that they will tell you that it was the uncertainty of it all that was the most difficult aspect. They might not say so in such a literal way, they may talk about the stress of it or the sleepless nights, but the underlying difficulty will have been managing the uncertainty of it all.

It paralyses us in ways that might seem silly, maybe you've seen the fans watching the football in the final minutes of an important game where the score is even, willing, hoping, even praying that their team scores a goal, the uncertainty is tangible and painful, and when the final whistle is blown there is release from it, which is either replaced with elation or disappointment, but at least the uncertainty is over. The unknown final twist in a movie can keep us enthralled, what will happen, will the main character triumph over adversity or will they perish? I can remember TV serials as a child when the episode would pause in full flight and "to be continued" would be flashed on the screen, we weren't to know what's about to happen, the anguish that the uncertainty would cause was almost too much to bear, so uncertainty can hook into us and we can at times almost buy into it.

People can also restrict and resist all kinds of events and experiences, as the uncertainty is too much to manage, too much to go through. Job interviews, exams, social encounters can all hold immense levels of uncertainty, "what will I say?", "what will they ask?", "what will they think?", "how will I cope?". The uncertainty fuels the doubts, which kicks in the worries, which pushes on our brakes and nothing happens, uncertainty avoided. Yet no experience had, which then leaves us even less able to tolerate uncertainty not only in general but, potentially, even less so than when we started to toy with the idea of the social gathering etc.

People can and do go to extraordinary lengths to attempt to try and ensure certainty from having organised wardrobes, scheduling the week, setting goals, to trying to predict the weather, trying to predict the lottery numbers, to trying to predict the major financial trends of the future. The effort that can be put into trying to minimise or even cancel out uncertainty is often more wearing, tiring and unhealthy than it would be to simply go through with whatever the event was in the first place. Excessive planning, excessive scheming, excessive fretting, excessively inventing strategies to employ in the event of anything from urgently needing to go to the toilet to being able to deal with sudden medical emergencies.

In such cases people build up dependence on "safety behaviours" which can range from carrying a bottle of water to more major things such as having a defibrillator in their car boot all in an effort to try and reduce the uncertainty and it's ensuing impact on us which is actually the most important thing. However, people build up such high levels of dependency on safety behaviours that they wind up generating even higher levels of uncertainty than there were to begin with. This is because there is an ever increasing number of things they feel they need to remember, so many things to fit in their bag, tablets to take, routes to plan, places to avoid etc.

Besides this, more so than at any other time in history, we have so many possessions, that make dealing with uncertainty harder not easier. For example, smart phones have made us more slaves and prisoners to them not the masters of them. In the past if we did not hear from people we would have somehow dealt with it, yet nowadays if we don't receive texts or calls at certain times and quite regularly we can soon leap to the conclusion that something is wrong. In the past we might have thought things through in a more balanced way and dealt with the uncertainty of not getting that call and not jumping to conclusions, although now things like technology have made us more susceptible to struggling with periods of uncertainty. This can lead us to excessively worry if things are ok at the moment and if they are going to be ok in the future. Not convinced? Just try leaving the house without your mobile phone, I know I can't. Also, the level of information that surrounds us in these days is immense, news, social media feeds, multiple streams of images, text and data coming at us from all angles. Yet, paradoxically, this doesn't lead us to a serene life of peace, rather it cranks up our feelings and can leave us hungry for more uncertainty inducing "information".

One tactic that people use to avoid uncertainty is staying in the good old safety zone. People can develop highly sophisticated routines, (they might not seem sophisticated on the exterior but they are) habits and patterns of behaviour that on the surface keep things ticking over nicely. Things seem to fall neatly into place and nothing threatening or sinister gets in and yes this seems to keep uncertainty at bay. However, these kinds of tactics actually decrease our ability to manage the "ifs and buts" of life, the distress and our ability to feel ok whilst life seems to be in limbo. Not only do the safety zone tactics diminish our ability to live with uncertainty, but, as with most coping strategies, they produce short-term solutions.

Short-term solutions are also a very significant minefield of suffering that people go through in an effort to overcome distress, pain or discomfort. Again, as with other areas, the cumulative suffering that short term solutions actually generate is likely to be worse for us than if we dealt with and confronted whatever it is the short-term solution seemed to cure in the first place.

The best example I know of the futility of short-term solutions is the person who is suffering from hemorrhoids. They continue to shuffle around in their chair trying to ease the discomfort which eventually works, temporarily that is, until the next time that the discomfort creeps back upon them, then they shuffle around again until things ease, but the discomfort comes back. They are far too embarrassed (understandably I guess) to visit their doctor to discuss this and to allow the doctor to see their bottom, yet if they were able to deal with this, it is highly likely that they would find a much more beneficial long term solution to their pain, suffering and discomfort.

Struggles with uncertainty go hand in hand with short-term solutions, yet short-term solutions create just that, short-term relief, short-term reduction in distress. Two further drawbacks with short-term solutions are that firstly it is inevitable that we won't continuously experience the same level of relief or resolve from our trusted old technique. The person mentioned above will need to shuffle more and more and also need to invent more believable excuses to cover up their shuffling.

Secondly, we will once again have begun to tolerate it, so we need a more effective short-term solution which by now is using up more effort, taking longer to invent and keep up than the period of relief that it brings about. Also, this repeated creativity of short-term solutions is, in the bigger picture of things, as counter productive as it can get. It is akin to papering over the cracks rather than dealing with re-plastering the entire wall, it is plugging the holes in the boat rather than going through the hassle and demands of making more effective long lasting repairs. It is also very rare that people will gather up and harness all their efforts and learning that they receive from devising multiple short-term solutions and weave them into a glorious long-term master plan.

Some repeated short-term solutions can work well in life, such as sleep, or washing and eating, yet when it comes to dealing with uncertainty and trying to eradicate it by whatever method, especially short-term, it is akin to trying to deny gravity! It can't be done, it is impossible, we have to come to the point at which we can accept uncertainty, become adaptable enough to reduce the impact of it, minimise the impact of it by confronting it, we take it on the chin. In basic terms, we live with it! We control the effects of uncertainty rather than it controlling us.

I hope the links with uncertainty and all kinds of

emotional struggles are clear, it is the feeling or the notion of the "unknown", whether that is created by excessively tuning into an apparent sense of breathlessness or, as previously mentioned, agonising over "what will they think of me?". This fearful perception of the unknown leads to intensified emotional and physical reactions, which lead to unhelpful behaviours, which have short-term benefits. These then become overly relied upon, become embedded, lead a person to do things that they would rather not resulting in them feeling low, isolated, misunderstood and unhappy.

In my experience feeling unable to deal with uncertainty is at the heart of many emotional struggles, yet this feeling very often occurs in a highly selective way. People can latch onto only certain factors that appear to increase the uncertainty, such as increased heart rate, for example, and then they can fixate on this until it becomes almost unbearable. This usually happens though at the sacrifice of acknowledging other real immense levels of uncertainty that we barely and conveniently even notice say once a year, let alone once a day. There are so many things that we take for granted which would become redundant with just the flick of a switch and which would have massive impact on us such as a power cut. A long time without electricity could bring about all kinds of difficulties for everyday life although consideration to this kind of thing gets left out and is conveniently replaced by things that are perceived to be more likely. Yet it's usually the case that the apparently uncertain things that people latch onto causing dread, are actually less likely, not more likely, to happen or occur. Overcoming the power and influence of uncertainty is key in enabling people to move on from all kinds of emotional struggles, as the disabling power of it often leads to significant issues with making decisions. Doubts creep in about doing the right thing, the most beneficial thing, the quickest thing and the least threatening thing. These doubts pollute our thoughts as we wrestle to turn them into thought equations that feel pleasing to us. It needs to be remembered though and I can't stress this enough, that uncertainty is a nemesis that cannot be defeated, it is as fundamental to life as day and night and the turning of the seasons, so the effort that goes into trying to overcome it is wasted. Uncertainty is as essential as the idea of winners and losers, somebody needs to lose so that there is a winner. Uncertainty needs to exist so that things can be experienced and perceived as certain. If we were to be somehow magically told that every single thing under the sun would suddenly become 1000% certain, how would that impact on how we deal with life? What if we were told that our cars would never again break down, we would never be ill, our partners would never leave us, we would always have a job, we would never have the need to experience fear, doubt or dread ever again. Surely this would lead us to fall into an awful malaise where life becomes so predictable, so routine, so obvious, so dull and potentially so dreary and truly depressing as nothing changes, nothing unexpected happens. How would life feel if there were no spontaneity, no surprises, surely we would become intensely complacent, switched off and zombified!

The great and fearless explorers have, throughout the history of the world, used uncertainty as fuel to get them through the challenges and the tests that they experienced. I wonder how motivated the first climbers of Everest would have felt if, at the start of the expedition, they would have somehow been given guaranteed assurances that they would definitely reach the summit. What would there be for them to overcome, what would the effort all be for, what would the purpose of the struggle and the fight be for? Just a bit of a jolly up Everest?

Uncertainty is a highly paradoxical aspect of life. We cannot experience certainty without uncertainty, and maybe the notion of certainty is truly just an illusion that we entertain ourselves with. Just like the idea of control, people who strive to achieve a sense of control through various behaviours and routines are potentially the people who are the least in control as, if they truly felt in control, they wouldn't need to relentlessly check their bank account or the locks on their doors. So maybe the idea of certainty is similar, it is an illusionary state that we pursue that somehow lulls us into a temporary state of serenity. Crucially though this experience of serenity is yet again temporary. Just think of all the effort that we might put into seeking out temporary serenity from the illusion of uncertainty only to wind up luxuriating in an equally temporary illusion of certainty!

The real key to dealing with uncertainty is that we are flexible with it and that we don't place too much emphasis on things being in a certain way, that we are able to adapt and deal with things as they come at us. Our physical bodies are so intelligently designed so that they are flexible, such as our expandable ribcages where our organs do not have a fixed space to work in, and that in the case of a car accident for example our ribcage can expand and move for protection allowing for movement in response to the impact. This is how we will best deal with uncertainty, allowing for movement, allowing for impact and being flexible.

Essential points to remember from Chapter Six

- Avoidance of uncertainty prevents new experiences from happening so nothing changes.
- Is it easier to go through with things than excessively trying to prevent them?
- Are you trapped in a safety zone?
- Short-term solutions don't work.
- Selective about the uncertain things that you tune into?
- Uncertainty is a nemesis that can't be defeated.
- Certainty and uncertainty are illusions.

Chapter Seven

Blame and expectations

"Love, praise and admiration offered and then snatched back with a condition……."

Chapter Seven
Blame and expectations

It is such a painful experience to sit opposite another person who is convinced that they are to blame for how things are. Especially so if they are upset whilst this happens, yet more painful still when they have become so convinced of this that even a therapeutic bulldozer would do no more than scratch the surface.

I'm not talking about being to blame for a theft or a death or an actual crime, (although I have been with people who have been sent to prison after being convicted of crimes that they and I knew they didn't commit), I'm talking more about when people feel that the way things are is their fault and because things are "their fault" it is a foregone conclusion that they are to blame.

Some examples would be that

"The family argue often and I should be able to stop it",

"I try as hard as I can although things still don't seem to improve so therefore it is me that is to blame",

"They have always said that it is because of me so that must be right, it has to be me to blame".

These examples are actually a little extended as it is very common for somebody to say something along the lines of the first section of these examples i.e. "I try as hard as I can but things don't seem to improve" the following section, the punch line if you will, "so it's me to blame" very often gets left out, it is unspoken, but it is very powerfully implied.

Maybe you don't need me to tell you that blame and pointing out our apparent faults seems more and more to be an international blood sport where very few are spared mockery, ridicule, embarrassment and humiliation. Perhaps it's me that is highly tuned to noticing this kind of thing but highlighting faults, dishing out blame and an obscene amount of emphasis on "lessons learned" seems to me to be ever more commonplace, more acceptable and less challenged than ever before. It feels to me that this is at such a high degree these days that we barely even notice it let alone question it, in fact if people weren't blamed, criticised or hauled over the coals then it might seem a little odd. Don't get me wrong, I'm not talking about such levels of irresponsibility where no-one is accountable for anything, not at all, I am talking, though, about a backdrop where an excessive emphasis on criticism, blame and flaws sets an intensely unhealthy scene for people to do well on. Maybe this is not breaking news but I still feel that it is extremely relevant and also goodness knows what would happen if somebody were to get praised!

I would say that there hasn't been a single person that I have treated where some element of self imposed blame or fault didn't put in an appearance at some point. This can of course hinder progress by itself, but it can also be intensified as blame and fault all fall nicely into line with our expectations. What a fortune I would have even if I had just one half of a penny for every time somebody said to me that they "should" be able to get over it, deal with it, sort it out, grow up, pull themselves together, stop being stupid, stop being pathetic, stop being weak, know what to do etc, etc, etc.

Our expectations set the benchmark for what we feel is acceptable or unacceptable. Acceptable or unacceptable behaviour, acceptable or unacceptable levels of coping, acceptable or unacceptable levels of "not coping", acceptable or unacceptable levels of just about everything under the sun! It's not only the expectations we have of ourselves that link into levels of self blame, it is also the expectations we feel that others have of us.

It is a true and very long held therapeutic notion that these kinds of expectations can often come laden with conditions, conditions that conveniently skew the original "intention" of the expectation. The best example of this that I have ever heard is, mother speaking to son, who stated that she will be really proud of him, once he gets that top barrister job that is, her pride is dependent on the job, it is conditional. The mother who congratulates her very diligent, piano practicing daughter by saying just imagine, what it will sound like with no wrong notes at all. Love, praise and admiration offered and then snatched back with a condition. Admiration, that is dependent on achievement, or rather the perception of achievement and the perception of achievement is based on, you guessed it, expectations!

Expectations are also such a fundamental part of people's struggles and an entire tome of work could be legitimately written about them (and probably has been) that it might be a little remiss not to fully focus on them here, although, I just want to point out the crucial role they play when it comes to self blame and self fault finding. They can and do go hand in hand with the standards that people feel they have to not only attain and adhere to but also continue to maintain. Even Shakespeare chipped in with the negative consequences of excessive expectations saying that "Expectation is the root of all heartache".

As with similar themes in this book, we are looking here at extreme expectations that are not realistic or sustainable, we are not looking at being without aspirations or ambitions at all. The essential point is that expectations are best for us when they are a driving force rather than something that sends the car careering out of control and ending up in a motorway pile up! Worse still that we wind up berating ourselves for having crashed.

I'm sure you get the message here about excessive standards and the likely outcome. Yet, as with most emotional struggles, this kind of thing gathers momentum and can turn into a way of life overnight. This happens, as I mentioned so many times already, before we even realise.

Also, excessive expectations don't always involve grand plans, lofty dreams or elaborate government toppling ambitions, they can also be highly debilitating when people apply them to the minutia of things. A convenient example of that is not the levels of attention applied to an entire essay that somebody might write, it could also be the sentence structure, or the punctuation or the precision of the points being made or even that hand drawn ruler lines are straight.

Many further examples of this can be found in instances where perfectionistic tendencies hold too much sway. Take the true story of the straight A student in the second year of her masters degree in politics. At the end of the second year her tutor realised that he hadn't received any course work from her at all. He contacted her to discuss this and he asked her where her work was and if she had finished it. "Oh yes, it's all finished" she told him and her course work was all there on her computer and that it had all been done and completed in its entirety just six weeks into the second year. Perplexed, he enquired as to why then hadn't she handed it in? There was a long pause, finally the reply was "Because. It's not good enough". The work was all finished, yet it just wasn't "good enough". I don't know how this conversation continued but I would hazard a guess that it may have gone on to contain themes of being to blame and being at fault fuelled by many unhelpful instances of excessive expectations, letting people down and falling below self imposed acceptable standards.

So the work was finished and it could have been handed in although the barrier to this was the thought that "it's not good enough" which is an example of a typical intro to a very unhelpful 'thought equation'. This intro might be followed by "I am to blame" which is a typical middle and perhaps "I can't cope" for example being a typical conclusion. Other typical conclusions might be "I am unloveable", "I am not likeable" "I will never amount to much" etc. This would be a classic example of an extremely faulty thought equation that can hold massive negative sway and influence.

Very often though, this kind of thinking equation is not put together in an arbitrary haphazard way, not a chance. I know that might sound unlikely or perverse but its true. I have seen literally thousands of people invest a terrific amount of effort, focus and concentration into establishing detrimental thought equations like these. They are made with carefully constructed beginnings, 'It is my fault" middles such as "I should, ought, must", and thus an end that fits like a glove i.e. "I am to blame" albeit though, an unhappy ending.

Obviously these kinds of thoughts don't do people any favours at all yet they are put together with great care and they are usually nurtured with high levels of attention and reinforcement. However, crucially and despite whatever effort may have gone into it, this kind of thought equation is very, very rarely based in reality, hard-core evidence or proof. Despite being seemingly well thought out, nurtured and often clung to, this kind of thought has its basis in assumption, speculation, prediction and poorly acquired "knowledge". Also this type of thought equation is often constructed in ways that are highly selective and choosy. Ways that conveniently do not acknowledge the full picture, ways that screen and filter out essential information along the way and that discount certain fundamental factors and essential elements. They also contain subtle devious ways to ensure that the reinforcement of a thought and belief like "I am to blame" is emphatically and consistently carried out and executed.

You see, all emotional struggles lead people to not only become increasingly myopic but also highly selective and picky in what they take on board. Highly selective, that is, about what gets through the mental immigration process, although, you might not be surprised to know that in this process there is a very common tendency to discount the positives. Surely you must have come across somebody in your life that has said to you that they just can't take compliments, well, this is discounting information 101. The compliment offered doesn't fit with how I view myself, therefore it cannot be allowed in, and furthermore it cannot be allowed access to the main control room or the motherboard. This might be followed by thoughts and beliefs that such access may tinker with my precious headspace which I know may not do me any favours, but it is the headspace that I cling to and I know that despite it's highly selective choosy and picky ways, I somehow survive with it, and it's all I have known for a long time. So, you, Mr. Therapist (or anybody for that example) are not going to take it away from me without a struggle, despite how much I appear to complain about it!

Thoughts and beliefs that generously fling around blame and fault are constructed thoughtfully yet oh so highly

selectively and they do a great deal of damage, yet they can be like precious gems that, perversely, people are reluctant to give up. It is the equivalent of continuing to eat something that you know will give you food poisoning, but still, it gets choked down somehow. That said though, it's not an automatic given that people ditch with great ease things that are not good for them.
In the film Castaway, Tom Hanks initially struggles to adapt to his new desert island surroundings and survival is very hard indeed, although he does overcome this and he masters his environment. However, he knows that he cannot stay there forever and that he needs to leave, yet leaving this way of life is painful for him and as he breaks through the tide and the waves to drift out into the sea he looks back at the island with sadness, loss and almost a sense of fondness. This often is comparable to overcoming emotionally debilitating things such as self-blame, it has become more than just a habit, it has become a way of life, familiar, and a rickety old stick that people lean on, just.

Tom Hanks struggled with his environment to begin with and the same could be said for an emotional environment that generates thoughts, which bring about self-blame and unhelpful excessive expectations. To begin with people may also struggle with them, even want to automatically reject them, yet somehow they become more workable and then they become the commonplace. However, something tells us that we can't live there forever, but leaving is an awful wrench.

Self-blame and an almost death wish level of wanting to

confer blame and fault onto self is how I see far too many people willingly put themselves in chains, lock themselves up and throw away the key. Undoubtedly rooted in low esteem and also very often linked with an absence of nurturing in younger years, self-blame is a hungry little thing that needs feeding often and as time goes on it demands higher quality food and increasingly regular feeding. The root causes of this kind of thing can be multiple and embedded, although, as this kind of emotional state develops, guess who the waiter, chef and restaurant owner usually is. I'm not saying that others don't make significant guest appearances and outstanding contributions to the menu, yet more often that not the restaurant is ever increasingly self-service.

A lack of acceptance in the findings for things being anything other than "my fault" are the initial target building blocks for overcoming this kind of thing. Rigidly held beliefs like "it always is" and "always has been my fault", "why would now be an exception" can at times provide significant barriers to progress. Yet experience is a first class teacher and the experiences gained through experience can leave long lasting impressions and scars. Impressions and scars that cannot be denied or ignored, as experience can never be cancelled out due to the essential role it plays in life and in our formation. Also bad, negative and debilitating experiences can linger longer in our minds and memories than is helpful and they can very quickly grow like moss and take root. Often they become deeply rooted and the task of digging them out becomes overwhelming, too much to handle and potentially not worth it. As I have inferred before, an overgrown moss ridden garden is better than no garden at all and living on a desert island might, at times, have its advantages.

Experiences and experience are the bedrock of our entire view of the world, it is our reference point for everything we ever do, think or feel. Also, it doesn't take many poor experiences to overthrow multiple good ones, of course, not all experiences are equally as powerful, either positively or negatively, yet the accumulation of bad experiences can and does wear us down.

So, if negative experiences can lead to self-blame and finding fault in ourselves, can't this be reversed? That would sound more than reasonable, although, it is a possibility that I see people very reluctant to explore. Why? Well, more often than not, because it might just happen again, I can't take the chance of being to blame again and next time it just might be worse and I might not be able to get over it if it is!

Therapeutic jargon would label this kind of situation as resistance or avoidance, and nothing, but nothing under the sun makes problems worse than avoidance. If you don't believe me just try it, avoid washing up the pots for a week and see how motivated you feel to deal with them! Resistance and avoidance are all very real elements of people's struggles when it comes to change. That said though, placing too much emphasis on avoidance and resistance as a barrier to change can be disrespectful to some of the very real fears that paralyse people who actually are brave enough to even think about considering change, being different and having a different way of life. The old adage goes that people don't like change and that is very, very true, but neither do people like dwelling in moss filled overgrown gardens. Life in overgrown, weed filled mental gardens leads to beliefs becoming fostered and nurtured by tunnel vision. This especially applies to negative beliefs that can be clung to for dear life at times, although, in this increasingly unpleasant emotional environment something usually has to give.

Arriving at the point of contemplating doing, being and thinking differently can be akin to arriving at that old familiar T-junction in the road. My expectations and things always being my fault and never feeling good enough have always made me take the same old bad choice at the junction, yet once again I feel compelled to take it. At this point the fight against the magnetic quality of taking the turn that has always been taken or being bold enough to drive down a new road and embrace the unknown is the heavyweight battle that occurs. The unknown is frightening and highly uncertain, yet surely not as frightening and truly uncertain as once again taking the turn at the T-junction that has been taken so many times, the one that leads to ever increasing erosion of how we are.

In simple terms, what is it going to be, the same old shit, or crazy new shit? Have you taken enough, or are you up for more self-inflicted punishment and torture. Moving on from self-blame and self-proclaimed fault begins with taking empowering choices and an openness to consider other possibilities, other reasons, causes and factors behind how things are and have become.

These choices are all bound up with worth, it is it worth it, am I worth it, will the unknown outcomes be worth it? The temptation to stay the same is immense, yet the moss grows ever fast and creeps further up on us without our even being aware. The levels of blame and fault also increase and the unhappiness remains. So, once again, what is it going to be? Have you truly had enough, are you truly worn out by unhelpful beliefs and behaviours or do you have room for a little more suffering and self blame?

Taking the first step of faith can be the hardest, especially the first step of faith in ourselves, yet that very same first step can open up the floodgates of our lives and allow our potentials to rise to the surface and lead us to flourish. The first simple step, so easy yet so scary, weighing up the possibilities either way, will I stay or will I go, will I allow myself to endure more pain and distress or will I choose to liberate myself. Thoughts and choices that can dictate so much of our futures, thoughts that can feel painful to have and to contemplate, yet at the same time thoughts and choices that can potentially alleviate so many struggles.

It has to be worth it and it is worth it, after all, what have you got to lose, what truly is the worst thing that could happen? If you want to make an omelette you have to break a few eggs. The riskiest thing to do in life is to not take any risks and nobody is ever to blame for being at fault for everything.

Believe that it will be worth it and the new experiences that you will have, will gradually erase the old ones, believe in the power of that simple first step, have a deep breath and take it, if you fall you can always get up again.

I have heard thousands of people tell me that in the end they were stronger than they realised, I truly believe this can apply to you, why wouldn't it? Surely, it would be awful for you to find out that you had much more in your locker than you thought when it is far too late.

Take your first step and see what happens, make your first liberating choice and see how you feel, take off your chains and feel the relief. I write this with intense faith in you and intense belief in how resilient we are.

I know that you can do it, let go of the blame, challenge your expectations and just take that first step. For you and nobody else, push the button, do it, now, right now, it will be worth it.

Essential points to remember from Chapter Seven

- Are your expectations excessive?
- Are you constructing unhelpful thought equations?
- Are you becoming increasingly myopic?
- Are you clinging to unhelpful beliefs?
- Is avoidance making things worse for you?
- Can you consider new choices?
- Can you take that first step?

Chapter Eight

Depression? Anxiety?

"What a revolution there would be if people stopped pathologising their lives and experiences and giving them self-polluting names such as depression and anxiety!"

Chapter Eight
Depression? Anxiety?

Maybe this is a good point to let you know that I don't like terms such as "depression", "anxiety" and "panic attacks". I know that this may be extremely controversial of me to say and I know that this may fly in the face of decades of research in to "mental illness" and diagnosis, but I base my ideas on real experiences at the cutting edge of therapy, significant anecdotal evidence and being relentlessly confronted with people in need, pain and distress.

Terms like depression and anxiety are far too often thrown around like confetti at a wedding and they are equally far too often latched onto and worn like badges, sometimes with a sense of shame, sometimes with a sense of pride! I have sat opposite many, many people who have been so low that they cannot leave the house, they cannot get washed and at times they do not want to live. So it may even seem cruel of me to say that I don't like the terms depression and anxiety. I will agree that I have seen many people feel horrifically low, in terrible anguish and distress yet I feel that terms such as anxiety or depression are actually incredibly disrespectful to the feelings, thoughts and experiences of those who are suffering. To me it is akin to telling somebody with the most dreadful migraine that they have a bit of a headache.

The terms anxiety and depression just don't do justice to the circumstances that people can struggle with. I'm saying, in a nutshell, that most terms that would get used in "mental illness" are inferior and that they play down and discount the humanness of the things that life throws at us. Terms like depression just lump all that people go through into a very narrow bracket and they give very little regard to the actual suffering that people go through. Things get simplified as being attributable to depression. I am almost in pain myself when I hear people say to me that they were "told" that they have "got" "depression" whether it is the doctor who said so or a friend who "knows a bit about this kind of thing". Yes, without doubt people do go through the most truly dreadful lows and awful woes and struggles, yet this idea of "getting" depression just does not acknowledge the spectrum of experiences that people may have had that has led them to get to the point at which that are decreed to "have" "depression".

The Diagnostic Statistical Manual version five (DSM V) is the international reference book for "mental illnesses" and it is an exhaustive directory of virtually every emotional struggle under the sun. It describes these struggles with a criteria list, a tick box exercise if you will, which, hey presto, leads to diagnosis. This again squeezes people's experiences into frameworks, which on the surface seem to sum up what that particular person is going through, although, people are not like cars, we can't be hooked up to a diagnostic tool that is able to identify with profound accuracy what the issues and difficulties are. Also, on this subject, the theory books that most trainee therapists have to read and study do not resemble what actually happens on the therapeutic shop floor, people do not usually fit what is in the books, the books, the theories and the interventions have to fit the person. A therapeutic suit is best when it is tailor made not bought of the peg.

The idea that we somehow "get" or "have" what people usually refer to as depression or anxiety gives the impression that we have encountered some form of virus or infection. For example, person A had five very close relatives all die within a year and now guess what she's magically got "depression"! No she hasn't, she is going through what any reasonable person would say is a very human response to such circumstances.

Depression for example isn't something that people just get, in the same way that we would get a cold, what is referred to as depression is more often than not, an extremely understandable, very natural reaction to the awful things that they have been through. Yet, there is a terrific reluctance to accept this, it is somehow easier to call it depression rather than calling it life, or calling it acceptable or, God forbid, calling it understandable. What a revolution there would be if people stopped pathologising their lives and experiences and giving them self-polluting names such as depression and anxiety let alone making this worse by subtly lording ownership over them, as in "I have X,Y,Z".

Such ownership is also a therapeutic battle at times, the very act of simply saying that I "have" depression is highly likely to lead people to feel lower, more down and more de-motivated, yet people still do it! Sadly, people also allow terms such as depression and anxiety to be the cause and even the justification for all kinds of things, I can't eat, therefore it is my depression, I can't sleep, it is my depression, I have lost my motivation, it is my depression. Yes, it is of course an acknowledged fact that what is usually referred to as depression can be extremely debilitating, yet, the essential point here is it being referred to as my depression, mine, I have it, therefore I own it, or, it owns me. Do people do the same thing with physical issues? Do they speak of cancer and tumours in the same way? Ok, so people talk of depression being an illness, maybe it is, although again this cancels out the essential paper trail of life that is likely to be highly significant. A person who has lung cancer may look back at all the years they smoked for and therefore have some perspective on the diagnosis, in my extensive experience this does not happen with "depression" or most other emotional battles. Instead people act as if "depression" is something that they get bizarrely inflicted with, something that they have, something that has taken over them.

A variation on ownership is when people spin this idea of "I've got" around and refer to it as "The" depression, as though it is out there like an entity that exists separately to them. It is out there like a sort of bad spirit that latches itself onto me and infects me. I have been in thousands of therapy sessions where the problem or problems, whatever they maybe, have been like a third person in the room. Neither the "I've got" or "The" methods of speaking about things are especially helpful as one almost welcomes the idea whilst the other is like an acknowledgement yet it also gently dismisses it. The most important thing is that this sense of either having got or living with "depression" gives credibility to what actually is an intangible thing and it can strip away our power to deal with what we are going through. The last thing that we need to do is to give power to any negative emotional struggle!

Let me make certain that you understand where I am coming from, I am not at all saying that people don't go through awful struggles and feel unimaginably low, (I know they do as I have seen this with my very own eyes) but I am saying that interweaving ones emotional struggles with inadequate, derogatory terms makes things so much worse. They simply just do not convey any regard for what that person has been through. Actually, they take the person, all they've been through, all the suffering, all the pain and whittle this down to 'depression". Funnily enough people tend to have much more pro-active and compassionate responses to say physical exhaustion, although, more often than not, especially with low mood, that is what has occurred, but it is emotional exhaustion! Yet I have a suspicion that physical exhaustion would be given a more sympathetic recovery plan, time to heal and compassion than the notion of emotional exhaustion.

The classification and categorisation of our experiences diminishes the reality of them and how they have shaped us and it consigns them to the unimportant file.

In the final analysis they get disregarded as unimportant evidence in the trial that happens in our own summing up. It is like putting make up over our scars. What an uncompassionate and highly disrespectful gesture it also is to all the twists and turns, losses and transitions that people have gone through, how they may have heroically persevered and trudged on, fought emotional battles over and over only to find themselves lumped with a bloody diagnosis of "depression"!

The term depression cancels out the legitimacy of our experiences, soldiers that go through battles and wars, who trudged through immensely dangerous territory are often rewarded at the end of this with medals and celebrated, yet people who go through the emotional equivalent are considered to have depression. The battles that are fought in the emotional trenches are equally as wounding and painful yet they are not given the same regard for the impact that they cause. I have sat opposite thousands of people that have been in the battlefield of life who have been emotionally shot at, attacked or bombed over and over again by things like death of a loved one, divorce or abuse. Eventually the final killer blow gets struck and they can't carry on, this is usually when, what is conveniently referred to as "depression", conveniently makes its appearance.

Little consideration is given to the debilitating events that may have led to feeling unable to carry on or cope, also at this point the emphasis is frequently on inability, not all the outstanding ability that people have displayed to get to that point. Often there is just bewilderment and confusion as to why the petrol tank is now empty and why the trip to the petrol station is incredibly difficult.

Giving disrespectful titles to the phases of our lives where we struggle is akin to muting out the minor sections in a symphony, it is the same as ripping out the pages in a novel where the hero gets wounded. You see what is commonly referred to, as being "depressed" is actually the clearest indication that people have actually been extremely valiant and endured so much. Yet, the frequent conclusion is that of failure and inadequacy rather than an acknowledgement of how strong and resilient they have truly been. It is beyond ironic that at the times in people's lives when they need to exercise patience, kindness and compassion to themselves they actually push the self-destruct button. Rather than giving consideration to all that they have coped with, dealt with and handled, the focus is frequently on inadequacy rather than outstanding world class resilience.

Take, for example, the long standing teacher of 45 years who has had a very successful career and was able to forge extremely productive relationships with the pupils, especially challenging ones. Due to work place politics he suddenly becomes unpopular and not the flavour of the month, a little further down the line an OFSTED observation gets skewed and he is labelled as lacking in skills. He is beyond belief with this and he is stunned that after all that he has given and offered he is viewed as potentially incapable. The injustice and the unfairness of it feels awful to him especially as he is months away from retirement. He feels unable to continue and his doctor signs him unfit for work, he also finds out that as a result of all this he may be released from his work contract. He is racked with emotional turmoil and feels dreadful, he has lost his livelihood, his purpose and hope for the future. He is defined by his doctor as having "depression", wham bam, just like that, after years of displaying immense ability, deftly dealing with life, he is consigned to the heap of the "depressed". Not that this is the doctor's fault, more so it is the concept of depression and it's all encompassing sway. His experiences, his multiple losses, his sense of purpose and source of hope all robbed unfairly, yet he now has "depression", yes, he may feel awfully low, lost and desperate, yet what an inadequate and inappropriate title to give to the accumulation of his experiences, and to top it all off he now "has" "depression"!

It is suggested that depression is the most growing problem on the planet and that it will soon be the biggest. Well, if that is true then the problem will be even bigger if the concept of it continues to be allowed to throw all our experiences into the mincer and spew out a definition of an all encompassing depression or any derivative of it. The kind of definition that, oh so subtly, implies that somewhere along the line, we weren't quite strong enough, we weren't quite hardy enough, we weren't quite up to the job. The definition surely should not be that we "have depression" but that we have "gone through LIFE"! As a result of being human and all that comes with it, certain shots and blows we took have wounded us, laid us low and taken chunks out of our hearts and minds.

Depression is the masher for the sum total of all our pain and distress, it takes our full colour experiences and turns them into negatives. The worst thing about the concept of depression is that it de-humanises all that is actually truly human, it cancels out our hurt and loss and further to this it often just adds to the pile of woes. Five of my close relatives have died within a year, which is bad enough, and now I've got depression!

I would strenuously encourage you never to lump all that you have been through into generalised and often convenient terms that simply do not acknowledge all that you are, all that you have endured and how far you have come. The culmination of your experiences may leave you feeling horrific, yet, I implore you to resist pinning all that leaves you to feel like this onto inadequate terms like depression and anxiety. It is more likely that you are an unsung hero, a outstanding example of bravery and a real Trojan who has endured the worst that life can throw, yet is still standing.

I'm not just saying this to be positive or to boost, I am saying it because in my experience of many thousands of times of scratching beneath peoples "depression" the hero is to be found. Perhaps trapped by the camouflage of deceptive terms and language but never the less still there. Doesn't being an unsung hero and a Trojan have a slightly more appealing ring to it than "having depression"? Over to you.

Essential points to remember from Chapter Eight

- Is it easier to call it depression rather than calling it life?
- Are you saying to yourself that you "have" depression?
- Are your labels diminishing what you have been through?
- Have you been through the battlefield of life?
- Are you lumping all your experiences together?
- Are you allowing "depression" to imply things about you that aren't true?

Chapter Nine

Obstacle courses and toolboxes

"So, there may be a little bit of bad news if you are trying to find just one way to get through life more easily, as it is doubtful that you will find the one single stand alone elusive magic technique......"

Chapter Nine
Obstacles and toolboxes

I have to admit that I am completely hopeless at DIY, I really can't even knock a nail in let alone saw or build or anything lofty like joinery! I have always been this way and I've never had the motivation, or need really, to try and improve in this area. It has caused a few problems along the way, led to repairs that could have been avoided and expensive paydays to make up for my lack of ability.

I am so relieved to say, though, that I do have quite a substantial set of skills when it comes to emotional, thinking and feeling work. I find that I am very thankful for this emotional toolbox and it comes to my rescue much more often than the tools that I have in my shed! Also the emotional tools that I have are interchangeable, so I haven't got a hammer that is simply just a hammer, I have a hammer that turns into a screwdriver and I have a screwdriver that I can turn into a pair of pliers, you get the idea. They are interchangeable as they are not fixed physical things like a plane or a chisel and as such they are not limited to single purposes or applications. So, my toolbox is varied and versatile, it has to be, because as I go through my own life I obviously don't find myself always trying to fix the same job or confronted with the same task. The jobs may have similarities yet I need to be able to adapt and adopt my tools and skills to fit the requirements and needs that have to be met. I get a lot of reassurance too from knowing that I have these "skills" that I can turn to, although, I also have to say that I've had to actively nurture and cultivate them over time, yet, this been more than worthwhile.

I feel these emo-tools have helped me with confrontation, disappointment, ups and downs, pessimism and many other emotional twists and turns, they also enable me to have a good perspective of things and to be able to see the bigger picture. So they're essential to me and the more I have found that I rely on them the more I never leave home without them. The tools that I have and would encourage you to own too are based on some of the themes in these pages. An easy example would be chapter five in that I don't let my own personal bottle of pop overflow, I have the equivalent of a bottle opener that I do use when I need to.

Besides needing a set of emotional tools to overcome things I also compare going through life with an obstacle course and that the various trials and tribulations we have to face could resemble the variety of challenges that you would need to be able to overcome on an actual obstacle course. You need to be able to climb the wall, shuffle through the tunnel, scale the rope net and balance on the see-saw plank and the tools that you assemble enable you to more successfully navigate the assault course.

So, there may be a little bit of bad news if you are trying to find just one way to get through life more easily, as it is doubtful that you will find the one single stand alone elusive magic technique or well, if you do please let me know! Just as you need to cook a meal, be a footballer and play the piano, several skills are required to complete the job or to stay on top of the task in hand. Moving on from dealing with low mood, emotional turmoil and personal struggles will require you to assemble a versatile and adaptable life tool-box and then you will need to learn which tools are needed for which job. In other words you need the emotional equivalent of a Swiss army knife.

When it does come to being practical and being able to fix, mend and repair things I am always in admiration and envy of my father-in-law, Alan. If I ever do feel able to attempt to try and carry out a little DIY, more often than not my approach is a little gung ho as I tend to just pile in there and try to make an impact! In doing so I make several mistakes along the way and usually leave behind more jobs to complete than I started with. Yet my much more canny father-in-law has the ability to stop, assess the problem and consult his substantial tool collection and select just the right tool or device to do the job. His more studious approach enables him to find the implement that is just right and more often than not he will take two, three or sometimes four attempts at this to ensure he has just the perfect one. Whether this is the gauge of a drill bit, the weight of a hammer or sometimes a mixture of more than just one, he is methodical enough to get this section of the job spot on, you see getting this part of the job spot on leads to a better outcome.

This has been a big lesson for me as I gradually realised Alan's style, how he assessed the job, stood back, thought about the potential difficulties and then chose the most ideal piece of apparatus for it to make dealing with the job as easy as possible on him. I will confess that over the years I have been in an emotional mess and reached for the totally wrong emotional "tool" to help me out and it has made things worse. A couple of quick examples would be feeling low and then isolating myself, feeling resentful and then allowing myself to dwell on things. Not good.

So, back to Alan, his approach is how I would encourage you to enable yourselves to move on from wherever you are right now. If you are down, distressed, desperate, low, uptight, inconsolable, worried, panicky or not feeling great in anyway, to move on your emotional tool box needs to be assembled with care and with quality tools that will last and serve you well.

You will need to try and acquire the most expensive tools that you can afford and also try to gather ones that come with a recommendation and ones that you feel will be reliable and not let you down just when you need them most. You might also need to have a tool shed at home, a tool box as you go around and maybe even a micro-tool kit that you can keep somewhere on your person as you go out and about.

Ok, I can hear you already asking what tools do I need to put into my emotional tool box? Well they are all there in theses pages. These suggestions are of course all metaphorical comparisons for you put your own stamp on.

Chapter One
Are you aware enough? Is your awareness like a blunt saw that needs its teeth sharpening?
Toolbox: A sharper saw.

Chapter Two
Are you telling yourself that you are the problem? Are you looking at yourself as the source of all that is going wrong?
Toolbox: A more accurate gauge.

Chapter Three
Over-thinking: Are you going round in circles thinking yourself to a standstill?
Toolbox: Just one very precise tape measure.

Chapter Four
The Rule Book: Walking through a laser beam maze? Yet triggering off the alarm?
Toolbox: A good wiring diagram.

Chapter Five
The Bottle of Pop: Letting your emotions get to boiling point!
Toolbox: A good thermometer or bottle opener.

Chapter Six
Uncertainty: What, if, when, how?
Toolbox: A simple note pad.

Chapter Seven
Blame and Expectations
Toolbox: A set of spare fuses (sorry couldn't resist).

Chapter Eight
Depression?
Toolbox: A quality guidebook.

Chapter Nine
The toolbox and assault course.
Toolbox: A toolbox and set of tools!

Chapter Ten
Always hope.
Toolbox: A set of reminders of your achievements.

The most important point I hope that you will take from this is that to seriously move on you firstly need more than one skill, tool, plan, technique or method to overcome how you may be feeling.

Secondly you need an interchangeable set of trusty and dependable "tools" that will work well in various circumstances and ones that can also be transferrable to different settings.

Thirdly, remember that it's an obstacle course that you are overcoming which will present differing challenges for you. So, for example, if you are feeling uptight you might need the equivalent of an emotional compass to find out where you are and what's going on and also a map to help you find your way out of the tension and confusion.

If you are feeling low, you might need the emotional equivalent of a sundial to find out where you might draw some energy from. You will need this miniature arsenal of strategies to lean on and to get you out of a spot and unfortunately one skill or method won't allow you to keep going and produce all the results you would like, not long term anyway. Very true, however, you might find that two or three trusty techniques which consistently serve you well, although, having a few more up your sleeve won't hurt.

Don't forget though, that the skills and tools, which, for example, help you scale the emotional wall of life, will have some transferable benefit to walking along the corresponding emotional seesaw without falling off. So the tools that you acquire and develop along the way will become multipurpose and not only good for one job or task. If you don't have such a set of skills to get by what will you be depending on? Just responding to the moment, gut instinct, acting with panic, knee jerk reactions? The whole idea of this chapter is to encourage you to pro-actively consider how you deal with emotional struggles and issues on an ongoing basis, are you always relying on your gut instinct, improvising and making things up as best as you can as you go along? There are endless actual comparisons in other areas of our lives, first aid kit in the draw, spare tyre in the boot of the car, spare fuses in the cupboard - do you have the equivalent for your moods, thoughts and feelings though?

So, you need to get ready to tool yourself up and get multi-skilled so that you are energised, enabled and empowered. Besides this you also need to ensure that the equivalent of any battery-powered things in your toolbox are regularly checked and not allowed to run down too much, especially the ones that you might turn to more than others. Your toolbox and the skill set that you develop for your own personal obstacle course will also need updating and it will need to be cared for and stay well maintained. The outcomes of each and every emotional obstacle that you overcome will be something that you can store and access whenever you might need to. Once you have assembled the basics of your toolbox you will always be able to build on it and hopefully the ideas, suggestions and themes in this book will give you a good starting point to work from.

Just in case you are reading this and thinking that you are too old to do or to need this, too mature to need a toolbox to cope, too young, too experienced, too intelligent etc, etc, etc well, feel free to carry on down that line of thinking and see how far you get. I would strenuously encourage you not to fall into that trap like so many thousands of people that I have seen, surely you wouldn't deny your body protein and vitamins, it is exactly the same thing with your emotions and feelings. If you like, I'm talking about a mental and emotional pantry, food freezer and snack box, how many goodies might most people stash in those places, how many treats might they give themselves, how many trips to the take-away, how many recipe and cookbooks might they read, how many conversations might they have with friends about their favourites and how much knowledge and information might they share and seek out about this kind of thing.

Ok, so, we all know that this can't be ignored right, and that physical starvation is not a great life style approach but the same does go for emotional starvation, malnourishment and poor emotional maintenance due to an empty toolbox or a lack of interest in owning one or one that's badly assembled.

Please do not overlook this crucial part of your life and to carry on the food example, you wouldn't poison yourself or eat out of date food or intentionally stick to a diet of junk food. You need to apply the same levels of respect to your emotions and feelings, they are equally, if not more, important and essential as the actual physical food that you put in your stomach.

It is essential that you embrace the idea of an emotional toolbox and also that you view overcoming things as an obstacle course. This dual emotional and practically based mix is something that will enable you to feel more competent at dealing with things and going through your own personal obstacle course increasingly unscathed. I wonder what your reaction would be to a plumber that turned up empty handed to mend your boiler asking if you could lend him a ratchet? Or how would you feel if an electrician arrived at your house without a wiring diagram asking you if you had a spare pen and paper that he could figure things out on. I assume you would be horrified that they weren't prepared or armed with any implements or apparatus, yet how many times might you leave the house or wake up trying to face the day in a similar way? Also any decent endeavour in life has at least one back up plan whether you are going to rob a bank or walk the dog.

I truly wish I could give you the single magic cure and a guaranteed one fits all solution to all your problems (the suggestions in this book are pretty good) yet there just isn't one. Sadly, life doesn't come with a manual or blueprint to deal with the things that get thrown at us so sometimes we have to learn on the job, although preparation and a readily assembled arsenal of skill, tools and methods will stand you in extremely good stead. Don't delay putting yours together now!

Essential points to remember from Chapter Nine

- Build a toolbox based on the ideas in this book.
- Think obstacle course.
- Emotional Swiss army knife.
- How Alan chooses the right tool.
- You do need an emotional toolbox.

Chapter Ten

Always Hope

"Hope resides in us, we are it, we are the walking warehouses of hope, it is not just a theme in a humanitarian song or an intangible fake concept that is used as a carrot to get by - we are it!

Chapter Ten
Always Hope

As I mentioned in my introduction, people can frequently ask whether or not I get negatively affected by *"listening to people's problems all day"*. My answer has always been the same and will be for as long as I am a therapist in that I feel immensely privileged to have the honour of being with people who are, in some cases, going through the worst parts of their lives. Why do I feel so honoured?

Well, there are a few reasons, firstly I am pretty much given access all areas to so many people's highly guarded thoughts and feelings and I have been able to journey alongside them as they/we try to find a way out of their emotional maze. I have sat with people who have been in floods of tears, people who have been terrified of having another nightmare, people who have been in sheer terror at the thought of answering a knock at the door, people who have been viciously abused by others and people who have felt beyond isolated and alone.

These kinds of experiences just don't happen everyday and most people are not privy to the depth, intensity and authenticity of the thousands of encounters that I have had. I have felt truly grateful to sit with people when the chips have, to say the least, been down and I feel that it can be easier to be with people when the going is good yet perhaps its not quite the same when people are beside themselves and in floods of tears desperately unsure of what the future might hold. Of course, though, I also have the extreme privilege of seeing people overcome tremendous hurdles, surpassing the fears that held them back, moving forward and breaking out of the chains that once bound them.

Alongside this and perhaps a moment that to me feels like even more of an honour, is when people tell me that I understand. They tell me that for years they have felt odd, weird, alone, freaky, stupid, mad, fucked up and for somebody else to be able to understand is monumental. The meaning to that person of somebody else understanding is immense. Somebody else understanding means I'm not going mad, I'm not a head case, I'm not an idiot after all and maybe I could put all of this behind me. The point at which somebody tells me that they feel I understand is super special indeed, it always feels like a truly unique experience and an extremely empowering one for the person who feels that eventually they have been received, heard, understood.

Alongside this is one of my treasured therapeutic concepts, that unless there has been some kind of psychological "movement" between both the patient and the therapist then it is possible that the content of the sessions may not have been especially impactive or effective. I feel I can say that movement, emotional that is, does frequently occur and that I do grow and develop in the sessions too. This though, involves making myself open, emotionally available and real, this is both scary and vastly powerful and to me it is often the pinnacle of human interaction, authentic human connections with no barriers or blockages, you see, I am a very lucky man to do this work.

If this weren't enough I have also been so honoured to see thousands of transformations, maybe they all haven't been earth shattering or government toppling, sometimes they have been subtle and slight. Often though, they have gone on to continue to influence more change after the sessions have ended and been like small acorns that have grown and grown. I have also seen many, many phenomenal changes where people who have been slaves and prisoners to their fears and doubts metamorphasise into world-beaters who go on to feel inspired to further enable others.

So, you might imagine that doing what I do is some powerful experience and you would be right. It is also edge of your seat stuff at times too as you never know from one session to the next what is going to happen and even sometimes from one minute to the next I don't know what somebody is going to say or what I am going to say back to them. I feel like I see real life, real issues, real pain and real experiences and the impact that others, life and challenges can have on people. It is a raw, radical and exceptionally real profession to have and I do feel truly so lucky.

All this said, though, it doesn't mean that at times it isn't also very difficult and demanding. Change, moving on and confronting fears is a complete emotional minefield, which can be prohibited by many of the things that I have mentioned throughout the previous chapters. I have never thought of giving up, never thought of calling it a day or changing careers. Why? Because the progress that people make, the virtual miracles that I have seen have been and still are a phenomenal source of hope. This relentlessly renews my faith not only in therapy but in the resilience of the human spirit and it's capability to overcome the most hideous of experiences and treatment. I have witnessed recovery from the lowest of lows, people who have been so traumatised and badly affected by what they have been through that I have sat opposite them and wondered how they would make it out of the hurt and emotional wilderness. But, they did! These experiences renew my hope, they remind me that hope is always there and that it never should be doubted, never frowned upon not even in situations that might seem totally hopeless.

These experiences where people do recover from the lowest of lows and find their way out of the darkness have shown me that there is an infinite source of strength, pliability and endurance in the human condition and in our souls and spirits which can be accessed as rocket fuel to blast us from the darkness into the light. The hammering that I have seen people take, either from others or self-inflicted, has been quite extraordinary at times. Multiple traumas, multiple abuse and multiple periods of suffering that have seemed insurmountable have gone from resembling the highest mountain range to a mere mole hill. How has this happened, well it could be attributable to the therapist or the therapy and maybe that all plays a part, although, I feel more than this, it is the tapping into the well of sustainability and strength that we have within us. Sometimes it is buried deep, sometimes it is frightened to come out and other times it is just brimming under the surface. Nevertheless, I know it is there and I have seen what happens when people tap into it and open the floodgates.

There is the story of the man walking along the sea front who sees something on a collection of rocks that appears to be like miniature palm trees, although upon closer inspection it becomes clear that it is actually seaweed! As he gets closer he views the scene and it is obvious that the rocks have been there for decades maybe even centuries and that the waves and the sea have battered the rocks and the seaweed consistently and relentlessly year after year after year. Yet, the seaweed has not been killed off, it has not shrivelled up or been defeated, not even by decades of never ending pounding. Not only this but the seaweed has also survived in extremely hostile conditions, living on rocks, pulverised by waves, yet it did not die. It didn't die, no, it did the opposite, somehow it thrived, it found ways to exist in the most unlikely circumstances and not only did it survive it actually flourished and it grew upwards and grew into something eye catching that resembled palm trees!

This true story is like a microcosm of the human spirit, a miniature example of how much can be endured and how adaptable the mind, body and soul are and if something as basic as seaweed is capable of this, what are we capable of? Debating the existence of hope is really not a debate at all to me, with my own eyes and ears I have seen and heard people overcome so many hurdles, fears and so much distress that I know that hope is real and is always there to be believed in. I can assure you that it is real and that it is not only the currency of the optimistic or the positive. Hope is not just a word or something that can be used to boost and motivate people, you see, we are hope personified. Hope resides in us, we are it, we are the walking warehouses of hope, it is not just a theme in a humanitarian song or an intangible fake concept that is used as a carrot to get by - we are it!

The philosopher Albert Camus in his book, The Stranger, said this:

"My dear, in the midst of hate, I found there was, within me, an invincible love.

In the midst of tears, I found there was, within me, an invincible smile.

In the midst of chaos, I found there was, within me, an invincible calm.

I realized, through it all, that...in the midst of winter, I found there was, within me, an invincible summer. And that makes me happy.

For it says that no matter how hard the world pushes against me, within me, there's something stronger, something better pushing right back."

You see hope is in the blood that gets pumped through our veins and it is in the thoughts, feelings and actions that will carry us through the most torturous periods of our lives. Hope isn't just the property of the financially wealthy, the scientist or the academic and neither is hope rationed or time limited. Hope is real and there to be tapped into, if it is conditional at all, the only condition is that the button has to be pressed, the step of faith taken to put the dream into action.

Hope is the engine within us, we just need to turn the key to hear it roar and roar it will! I have seen this over and over and I am not being excessive or attempting to be motivational.

I have seen hope in action, not just once or twice, no, thousands of times and in places where hope appeared to have left town.

My faith in hope is based on my real experiences and hope has gone on to reinforce hope, once it finds a way to come to the surface and influence things, it catches fire and the unimaginable becomes reality. If I hadn't experienced this repeatedly maybe I would have considered a career change, maybe I would have given up and maybe I wouldn't be writing this, yet I didn't, I haven't and I am. I am doing so to let you know what I see and hear, so that you may be able to take the insights that I feel I have gained and use them as a source to kick start your own hope in hope.

Maybe as you are reading this you are discounting the relevance of this to you and maybe you are thinking that others may have done well but that you would be the exception. Well, guess what, that's what many of the thousands of people that I have seen over the years have said too. Not me Ian, I can't, why would I be the one etc, etc, etc. Well, hope is not selective and it does not prejudice people it is not exclusive or elite, it is in abundance if you simply take one deep breath and give it a chance, a chance that will go on to change things if you just put one step in front of the other.

The belief I have in people and in hope has come from the people themselves, I have always been a very optimistic man although the hope and optimism that I have has been bolstered and consolidated by the transformations that I have seen.

My source of hope is, if you will, hope itself and that hope is real, alive and available, not just to the chosen ones, the elite or select few but to you and to me.

Whilst we are on the subject of hope, it is my sincere hope that you will benefit in someway from the themes, ideas and suggestions that I have written about. They are all based on real experience and real people's trials and tribulations as they have endeavoured to overcome their struggles and issues.

I hope that you might find even just the slightest element of encouragement and maybe the tiniest of a spark that will ignite your own life and your own hope in hope and in you. I can assure you that everything I have written is authentic and that this book is not in anyway a histrionic attempt to motivate you based on hyperbole and spiel, my experiences as a therapist have been intensely real and it has been my intention to copy that in these pages.

So, I can tell you that hope, change, progress, development, improvement, recovery, transformation and potential are all extremely true aspects of life which are right there to be grabbed and used as the crusading catalysts that they are. I would encourage you to never doubt yourself, never be afraid but to run towards the threat, run towards the danger and feel the excitement as you do.

Hope is as real as the air all around us, so go ahead and fill your lungs, go ahead and breathe it in and as you exhale know that you will be ok, things will be ok and that you will cope and overcome all that you are confronted with. You will, you will, you will!

Essential points to remember from Chapter Ten

- Hope is always there.
- Tap into your well of sustainability.
- We are hope.
- No matter how much the world pushes, you will push back.
- Hope is real.
- Hope is not selective.

IAN BEST

Disclaimer

(1) Introduction

This disclaimer governs the use of this book. [By using this book, you accept this disclaimer in full. / We will ask you to agree to this disclaimer before you can access the book.]

(2) Credit

This disclaimer was created using an SEQ Legal template.

(3) No advice

The book contains information about Therapy and common mental health conditions. The information is not advice, and should not be treated as such.

You must not rely on the information in the book as an alternative to medical from an appropriately qualified professional. If you have any specific questions about any medical matter you should consult an appropriately qualified professional.

If you think you may be suffering from any medical condition you should seek immediate medical attention. You should never delay seeking medical advice, disregard medical advice, or discontinue medical treatment because of information in the book.

(4) No representations or warranties

To the maximum extent permitted by applicable law and subject to section 6 below, we exclude all representations, warranties, undertakings and guarantees relating to the book.

Without prejudice to the generality of the foregoing paragraph, we do not represent, warrant, undertake or guarantee:

- that the information in the book is correct, accurate, complete or non-misleading;
- that the use of the guidance in the book will lead to any particular outcome or result; or
- in particular, that by using the guidance in the book you will [specify result] [or [specify result].

(5) Limitations and exclusions of liability

The limitations and exclusions of liability set out in this section and elsewhere in this disclaimer: are subject to section 6 below; and govern all liabilities arising under the disclaimer or in relation to the book, including liabilities arising in contract, in tort (including negligence) and for breach of statutory duty.

We will not be liable to you in respect of any losses arising out of any event or events beyond our reasonable control.
We will not be liable to you in respect of any business losses, including without limitation loss of or damage to profits, income, revenue, use, production, anticipated savings, business, contracts, commercial opportunities or goodwill.

We will not be liable to you in respect of any loss or corruption of any data, database or software.

We will not be liable to you in respect of any special, indirect or consequential loss or damage.

(6) Exceptions

THROUGH THE EYES OF A THERAPIST

Nothing in this disclaimer shall: limit or exclude our liability for death or personal injury resulting from negligence; limit or exclude our liability for fraud or fraudulent misrepresentation; limit any of our liabilities in any way that is not permitted under applicable law; or exclude any of our liabilities that may not be excluded under applicable law.

(7) Severability

If a section of this disclaimer is determined by any court or other competent authority to be unlawful and/or unenforceable, the other sections of this disclaimer continue in effect.

If any unlawful and/or unenforceable section would be lawful or enforceable if part of it were deleted, that part will be deemed to be deleted, and the rest of the section will continue in effect.

(8) Law and jurisdiction

This disclaimer will be governed by and construed in accordance with English law, and any disputes relating to this disclaimer will be subject to the exclusive jurisdiction of the courts of England and Wales.

(9) Our details

In this disclaimer, "we" means (and "us" and "our" refer to) [individual name(s)] of [address(es)].

OR

In this disclaimer, "we" means (and "us" and "our" refer to) [individual name] trading as [business name], which has its principal place of business at [address].

OR

In this disclaimer, "we" means (and "us" and "our" refer to) [company name], a company registered in [England and Wales] under registration number [number].

OR

In this disclaimer, "we" means (and "us" and "our" refer to) [business name], a partnership established under [English law] having its principal place of business at [address].

Printed in Great Britain
by Amazon